DEAD HEAD

DEAD HEAD, an original screenplay by Howard Brenton, was first broadcast by BBC-TV in spring 1986.

'The narrative was deliberately close to parody, even if those elements of caricature were placed rather disconcertingly within some very realistic scenes from contemporary life.

The effect was like that of a comic strip brought violently to life ... the first episode became a panorama of urban grotesquerie.'

Peter Ackroyd, *The Times*

HOWARD BRENTON

Howard Brenton was born in Portsmouth in 1942 and educated in Chichester and at St Catherine's College, Cambridge. In 1966 he joined the Brighton Combination as an actor and writer, and in 1969 he joined David Hare and Tony Bicât in Portable Theatre. His first full-length play was *Revenge* (1969) which was performed at the Royal Court Upstairs; this was followed by *Hitler Dances* (1972); *Magnificence* (1973); *Brassneck* (with David Hare, 1973); *The Churchill Play* (1974); *Weapons of Happiness* (winner of the Evening Standard Award, 1976); *Epsom Downs* (1977); *Sore Throats* (1979); *The Life of Galileo* (from Bertolt Brecht, 1980); *The Romans in Britain* (1980); *Thirteenth Night* (1981); *Danton's Death* (from Büchner, 1982); *The Genius* (1983); *Desert of Lies* (1983); *Bloody Poetry* (1984); and *Pravda* (with David Hare, 1985, winner of the London Standard Award, the City Limits Award and the Plays and Players Award).

The cover photographs from the BBC-TV production of Dead Head *show Denis Lawson as* Eddie Cass *and Lindsay Duncan as* Dana. *The pictures were taken by Willoughby Gullachsen and are reproduced by courtesy of the BBC.*

DEAD HEAD

A Thriller for Television

HOWARD BRENTON

A METHUEN PAPERBACK

A METHUEN SCREENPLAY

First published in 1987 in Great Britain as a paperback original
by Methuen London Ltd, 11 New Fetter Lane, London EC4P 4EE
and in the United States of America
by Methuen Inc, 29 West 35th Street, New York, NY 10001

Copyright © 1987 by Howard Brenton

Printed in Great Britain by Richard Clay Ltd, Bungay, Suffolk

The photographs of the BBC-TV production of *Dead Head* were taken by Willoughby
Gullachsen and are reproduced by courtesy of the BBC.

British Library Cataloguing in Publication Data

Brenton, Howard
  Dead head: a thriller for television.
  I. Title
  822'.914   PR6052.R426
  ISBN 0-413-15180-8

Introduction

> Do not forget that you are a nocturnal amalgamation of caves, forests, marshes, red rivers populated with huge and fabulous beasts who devour each other. It's nothing to show off about.
>
> Jean Cocteau

While I was writing *Dead Head* I had vivid dreams that the scripts were being dictated to me.

I dreamt that I was holed up in a foreign city, broke and alone. It was winter: the city was New York, but sometimes a New York that was devastated like the worst areas of West Beirut (where I had been during the Israeli bombing and siege of 1982 – an experience that has been trying to come out in my plays every since). At night snow fell amongst the ruins.

In this dream urban hell I was sitting in a bar late at night scribbling in a notebook. And Eddie Cass, the hero of *Dead Head*, came up to me. In the simple version of the dream Eddie buttonholed me, a bar-room bard bent on telling his story. In the grander, more confused Hollywood version Eddie, cigar in mouth and cocktail in hand, wreathed in a huge fur collar that seemed to make him float, hired me as 'a penniless bum' to ghost his autobiography for him. Through a kaleidoscope of dream-scenes I was by a Californian pool, an old typewriter before me (that one went nightmarish, I sweated a kind of red jam that clogged the keys); then I was in a hotel bedroom of furs, everything was coloured pale blue and Eddie lay on the bed naked with a woman, laughing at me.

I picked up tremors that high-placed BBC executives were jumpy enough that I was writing a series, because of my pen's somewhat spurious reputation for 'sex 'n' violence' – I didn't let on that I was also *dreaming* the bloody thing. English writers are wary about owning up to the demoniacal, instinctive origins of their work. To have 'a demon' is considered suspect: for professional reasons you pretend your work is wholly rational.

Two years on, the one scene I can remember that definitely came from the subconscious mind-moil was the very last. Eddie and Dana, paid off by the authorities, speak directly to the viewer from the balcony of the hotel in the Bahamas which they have bought with their 'nest egg'. It is as if the series has been a tall story told by an ex-con to a holiday-maker on a package-deal veranda in the sun. I'll claim this for Eddie's story – it is no taller than the Ancient Mariner's in Coleridge's poem. (What? The dead crew hoisted the sails, eh?)

The oddity of tall stories is that you tell them and then they turn out to be true. Since *Dead Head* was written there has been a stream of news items about faceless authority traducing individuals. The strange affair of the Stalker Enquiry is in progress as I write this. There have been the revelations of Clive Ponting and Sarah Tisdall, the untrustworthy information about the irradiation of North Wales and Cumbria, the doubts about the evidence against the prisoners sentenced for the IRA bombing in Guildford.

I was accused by some of 'paranoia', ludicrously because Eddie's predicament is obviously a deliberate reworking of the old joke: 'You're not paranoid. People *are* trying to kill you'. But I begin to wonder whether 'writer's paranoia' may actually be a finely-honed critical tool. Or maybe the bizarre sense of prescience that writers have – you write something, it happens – is not prophecy, it's simply that the human animal is so infinitely resourceful in its behaviour that if you imagine a story that in any way 'rings true' you can be assured that somewhere on the planet men and women are actually living it.

In the first draft, half of the series was set not with Eddie but with the committees of the Intelligence Agencies who monitor and manipulate his progress. Rob Walker, *Dead Head*'s director, objected that seeing the pursuers at work made the script 'too ordinary'. He was right, I threw out half of it, all the 'committee scenes' (the 'war-room' glimpsed in episode three is all that remains of that material) and rewrote.

By staying with Eddie throughout I abandoned the playwright's overview. I was free of the phoney Olympian certainty that ruins so many plays. I could now write Eddie's experiences 'from below'. Eddie asks, like Michael Kohlhaas, 'Why me?' From that simple question all his adventures flow.

I am indebted to an excellent cast, but must mention Denis Lawson's performance as Eddie. Denis, though a Scot, caught that South London wariness, the wry, flinty glance, confident but vulnerable – a look that says 'What's coming out of the wall at me next?' The part is sparely written and reactive – but Denis drew out with great skill and wit all of my hero's virtues: a humorous passivity that masks the toughness of a born survivor, a talent for improvisation, a ferrety persistence, a self-deprecating realism about himself and an innocent wonder at his adventures. Eddie is an Everyman wandering, on the viewer's behalf, through strange escapades in high and low places, struggling to believe that his worst fears are true.

Howard Brenton

Before Howard started on the text I took him to see DOA (*Dead on Arrival*) and *Gun Crazy*.

The broad elements of *film noir* are well known: the morally equivocatory hero groping blindly along the night streets as the rain sleets down; the women of uncertain commitment; the inexplicable menace from unexpected quarters and, forever, the teeming, dangerous city. Howard's text seemed to strive to impose this template on to Thatcher's gutted England with sometimes astonishing parallelistic force. I sought to force the parallels in no discreet manner; if we were to remind the viewer of those powerful antecedents then let the broad shoulders, high-style make-ups, battered trilbys be evident as a Brechtian signature on each scene.

The characteristic lighting of *noir* films is sometimes ascribed to the fact that, since many of them were low budget and made at speed, the placement of one or perhaps two lamps at studio floor level was simply the fastest way to work. Whatever the reason, a rich expressive range of lighting, sharply influenced by pre-war Expressionist film images, was developed through the forties. In *Dead Head* our aim was to deploy that cinema language, comment on it, quote from it and, sometimes, to ironise it. Because the programme was recorded on tape and film, special difficulties were encountered. The tape components sought, in essence, to imitate film. In all, four different people were responsible for the lighting. That a degree of homogeneity was achieved in this area is a tribute to some remarkable craftsmen.

The collision of demands of tape and film (a bizarre confluence of techniques that only the BBC utilises) seemed to me to be met with extraordinary ingenuity and skill by the BBC staff responsible. The BBC is an eccentric organisation with a huge well of talent, professionalism and expertise. The management are less expert at releasing that wellspring of talent into programmes.

The single play on TV has been relegated, by management parsimony and failure of nerve, into a cultural ghetto. The consequences are likely to be dire in terms of new writing. *Dead Head*, however, sought to inhabit the popular ground of the *Bergeracs*, the *Dynastys* and the mini-series. The impulse behind its conception was that the thriller form and structure could be harnessed to reflect the wretched particularities of Thatcher's Britain.

Dead Head was recorded during the bitter winter of 84/85 in 20 days filming, 10 days studio (tape) and 4 days location taping, called OB.

Robert Walker

'I would but find what there's to find, Love or deceit.'
W.B. Yeats

Episode 1

Why me?

Dead Head was first broadcast by BBC-TV in spring 1986. It was produced by Robin Midgley and directed by Rob Walker.

Episode 1

Characters

EDDIE CASS	Denis Lawson
DANA	Lindsay Duncan
ELDRIDGE	George Baker
HUGO SILVER	Simon Callow
CARACTACUS	Norman Beaton
JILL	Susannah Bunyan
POLICEMAN	Don Henderson
STOKER	Larrington Walker
SLEEPER	Winston Crooke
PUBLICAN	Forbes Collins
RED-FACED POLICEMAN	Peter Attard
WHITE-FACED POLICEMAN	Barrie Houghton
YOUNG WOMAN	Edita Brychta
TAXI DRIVER	Neil Munro
NEWSPAPER-SELLER	Eric Francis

i EDDIE: 'Stoker. One of those guys who just suddenly appear around the place like they've always been there. 'Bout whom you know nothing.'

ii STOKER: 'Look, I could put something your way, you know.'

iii PUBLICAN: 'You are barred from this pub.'

iv EDDIE: 'In twenty-four hours, how far can you go down?'

v EDDIE: 'What are you, their whore?'

DANA: 'You wanna break my arm? You wanna cut my head off, put it in my hatbox?'

1. Blank screen.

EDDIE (*voice over: South London, working-class voice. Very close to us. This quality of sound remains throughout his commentary*). What I want to know is, still want to know is – why me? Why me? Why did the world have to go mad round me? I mean – *my* world?

A pause.

It was Prince William's birthday, wan't it. I went in for an early pint, to drink the little Prince's health. The Lord Castlereagh, Peckham.

2. Interior. Pub. Early evening.

Few customers. Eddie at the bar, on a stool.

PUBLICAN. Eddie.

EDDIE. Benny.

PUBLICAN. Usual?

EDDIE. I'll have a Bell's on the side.

PUBLICAN. Special day?

EDDIE. For they who are loyal.

Close to Eddie, as he speaks voice over.

EDDIE (*voice over*). Always been a bit of a royalist. When I was a kid and my mum's Coronation mug got the handle broke off – I cried. It means a lot to me. Sort of – the Queen's somewhere in a garden. With flags. White horses. Having tea, cucumber sandwiches, tea out of a silver teapot. A kind of paradise – there in the back of your head.

And he has the drink before him. He raises his glass in a toast.
   Look at a picture of Prince Charles, Princess Diana and the baby Prince William, a colour photograph, framed, amongst the bottles and glasses behind the bar.

(*Voice over.*) There was nothing special about me. I had the average troubles. With the average memories.

Cut at once to:

3. Interior. Dana's flat. Night.

Eddie's wife's flat. It is in a Peabody Building. It is badly furnished and in a mess. A radio plays pop music from Capital Radio. A very drunk Eddie is in mid-row with his wife, Dana. She is hitting him in the face.

EDDIE. We are bloody married!

DANA. Not for long, you bastard!

EDDIE. What am I meant to do? S'all unfair! I just wanna be loved, thas' all!

DANA. Get out! Get out!

Cut back to:

4. Interior. Pub. Early evening.

Eddie sipping his pint.

EDDIE (*voice over*). Just like anyone else, really. Scraping the odd shekel.

Cut at once to:

5. Interior. Fish and chip shop. Night.

The Indian proprietor and his wife stand silently as Eddie takes the top off a large plastic bottle of domestic bleach and pours the bleach into the vat of oil. Clouds of steam and smoke rise from the vat; Eddie flinches and throws himself back. Through the steam and smoke, the proprietor and his wife stand impassively. They are used to this kind of incident. Eddie waves at them angrily. Without hesitation the proprietor goes to the cash register, rings up a 'No Sale', takes out ten five pound notes and holds them out to Eddie, who takes them, with an attempt at a friendly nod.

EDDIE (*voice over; over the above incident*). I am not a knight in shining armour. On one o' the white horses at Her Majesty's garden party, never pretend I was, I mean, we all have to get along, the grey reality, I mean – life being what it is. And all that. Times we live in.

Cut back to:

6. Interior. Pub. Early evening.

Eddie is just finishing the sip of beer. He

*licks his lips, sighs with satisfaction.
Then he takes a quick sip of the Bell's
whisky.*

EDDIE (*voice over*). What I want to get
through to you is, that where I come
from, I am Mr Average. Forget all
these bishops, blowing their mouths off
about 'the new poor' and 'the other
Britain' – I am British, I come from
Britain and that's that. My life was
average British. Though, I will admit, I
am prone to the average little cock-up.

Cut at once to:

7. Exterior. Garage. Night.

*The garage is in an archway under a
railway embankment. The mouth of the
archway is blocked by a grilled fence. A
barking alsation dog is jumping up at the
fence. Eddie and Caractacus, a black
Jamaican with rasta hair, are panicking
before the fence and the dog. Caractacus
is laughing.*

CARACTACUS. Hey dog! Dog! Hey dog
is God spelt the other way round –

EDDIE. F'crying out loud Caractacus
where's a meat!

CARACTACUS. Don't you panic boy, I
got the meat, an' you dog! I got the
meat –

EDDIE. Give it me then!

CARACTACUS. Meat! Meat! Hey –
here –

*He takes the meat out of his jacket
pocket.*

EDDIE. What am I doin', oh what am I
doin' here – (*He stops. Stares at the
meat in his hand. Sniffs it.*) This meat
stinks!

CARACTACUS. I poisoned that meat!

EDDIE. What? (*Sniffing.*)

CARACTACUS (*laughing*). That white
dog – is going to die!

EDDIE. What you poison it with?

CARACTACUS. Dettol, boy!

EDDIE. Dettol?

CARACTACUS. Soaked that meat, two
days and night, in dettol from the toilet –

EDDIE. Jesus Christ! Here, Doggie!
Doggie!

*The dog going mad, Eddie tries to
poke the meat through the fence. He
rattles the fence. An alarm goes off.
Eddie's fingers are snapped at by the
dog. He pulls his hand back.*

CARACTACUS. Hey man, what's going
down – the dog, the bells! Time to split
boy!

Cut back to:

8. Interior. Pub. Early evening.

*Peacefully, Eddie is drinking half the
pint. He puts it down deliberately, then
takes a breath and breathes out. Then the
voice over:*

EDDIE (*voice over*). Yeah. The odd
brush with society. Or whatever.

Cut at once to:

9. Exterior. Doorway. Night.

*Eddie is in the doorway, waiting
nervously. The sound of a car pulling up,
the light of a police car's flashing light,
the slam of a car door. A big and fat
police constable joins Eddie in the
doorway. The policeman has wide pores
on his nose. Look at his and Eddie's
faces closely.*

POLICEMAN. Hello, Eddie.

EDDIE. Hello, Malcolm.

POLICEMAN (*sniffs*). Dettol. You
get that?

EDDIE. What? No – I mean, someone
must've put it down round here.
Y'know. Hygiene.

POLICEMAN. Why would they do that?
You been pissin' on the walls, Eddie?

EDDIE. Na, let it alone Malcolm –

*The policeman suddenly puts two
fingers down Eddie's throat.*

POLICEMAN. Now I have heard a funny
rumour. 'Bout your eatin' habits. Prime
rump steak, marinated in dettol? You
are getting out o' your class, old son.
You should stick to fish 'n' chips –
bleached, eh? (*He lets go of Eddie's*

face.) While we are on fast food, you got something for me?

EDDIE. Yeah. Yeah.

Eddie takes out the ten five pound notes. Quickly and expertly, in front of Eddie's nose, the policeman takes six of them and then rolls up the remaining four notes.

POLICEMAN. How's your old lady?

EDDIE. We broke up. Months ago. You know that.

POLICEMAN. So I do. She is into some odd company these days.

EDDIE. Don't see her.

POLICEMAN. Out of touch? (*He tut-tuts.*) What a modern life-style you do lead, old son.

He pushes the notes into Eddie's mouth.

POLICEMAN. Don't get jumpy, Eddie.

Cut back to:

10. Interior. Pub. Early evening.

Eddie is putting an empty glass down. He takes a slug quickly from the whisky.

EDDIE (*voice over*). Yeah. Part from the royal occasion, it was just another Friday night. At the end of just one more week.

(*Speaks:*) All you need is love.

PUBLICAN. Pardon?

EDDIE. Nothing. Memory Lane.

PUBLICAN. Well, there you go, Eddie. (*He lifts the pint and whisky glasses.*) Same?

Eddie nods. At once:

STOKER (*off*). That will be my pleasure.

Eddie turns. Stoker is easing himself onto the stool next to him. Stoker is a thin, smartly dressed black Jamaican, elegant and at ease. He wears a black eye-patch.

EDDIE. Stoker! Where you spring from?

STOKER. One would like to reply, out of the violent night. Actually, from a pissy afternoon, failing to collect certain rents from certain properties.

EDDIE. What's all this with the eye?

STOKER. You like the pirate's patch?

EDDIE. It's bloody ridiculous.

STOKER. You have no taste, Eddie. No sense of style.

EDDIE. Someone bop you one?

Stoker looks around the bar then pulls the patch away from his face. There is nothing wrong with his eye. He winks.

EDDIE. Ridiculous.

STOKER. A little disfigurement. Makes you all the more attractive. You should try it Eddie. Brighten up your image.

EDDIE. Actually I've been thinking of going round with a false, wooden leg. I mean anything to make people love me. Na, I'd just get woodworm.

STOKER (*to the Publican*). Ben?

The publican approaches.

STOKER. Look the other way, Eddie.

Stoker and the publican exchange brown envelopes, quickly, each without expression. Eddie glances at Stoker.

EDDIE (*voice over*). Stoker. One of those guys who just suddenly appear around the place like they've always been there. 'Bout whom you know nothing.

Look at Stoker's right hand.

With that bit o' flash. Like his rings. You had no idea what he was into. I mean – why ask about people? I used to ask myself.

STOKER. Depressed, Eddie?

EDDIE. Could say that.

STOKER. Woman? Money? Little doggies biting your fingers?

EDDIE. Yeah. Well. (*He drinks.*)

STOKER. Look, er, I could, er, put something your way.

EDDIE. Too much is going my way these days.

STOKER. No. For real. I want to do this for you. (*Low.*) I mean. Five hundred pound. Absolutely. For nothing.

EDDIE. No.

STOKER (*insistent*). Not thieving. This is a job. More – a task.

EDDIE. Task. (*He nods.*) You do it.

STOKER. I would. But I have to be in New Cross at half-seven tonight.

EDDIE. Tonight –

STOKER. Oh yes! This is to be done tonight. You will have the money in, what, two, three hours?

EDDIE. What kind o' – task?

STOKER. All you do is – (*He takes out a piece of card.*) Go to this address.

EDDIE (*looks at it*). Kennington.

STOKER. S'a tower block. You pick up a parcel and –

EDDIE (*a little laugh*). Oh no, no.

STOKER. And *take* the parcel to *this* address. (*He turns the card over.*)

EDDIE (*reads it*). Regent's Park West? Bit out o' my class up there –

STOKER (*an urgent, tense edge is coming into his voice*). The only thing, don't take taxis. Bus, tube, or walk. Here's a hundred. (*He takes out five twenty pound notes.*) You'll get the rest at Regent's Park.

EDDIE. This is drugs in't it Stoker?

STOKER. Honest to God it is not. Look, this is just one thing, one thing.

He slides the twenty pound notes on the bar, under Eddie's hand.

EDDIE (*voice over*). Maybe there is just one split second of madness. In a lifetime. For each of us. It's there –you say yes or no. And that is your life – done. Decided.

EDDIE (*speaks*). OK.

Eddie's hand, sliding skilfully off the bar, the money in his palm.

Give us the addresses.

STOKER (*interrupting. A feverish light in his eye*). No. (*Flips the card up.*) Memorise.

EDDIE. Na –

STOKER. Four hundred quid coming to you. And you have no idea who you are doing a good turn, brother. No idea.

EDDIE. Bullshit –

He stares at the card, in Stoker's fingers. Then touches it – Stoker flips

the card over, with the affectation of a poker player.

EDDIE (*voice over; this over Eddie memorising the address*). Later that night, what I would have done for that bit o' card. Typed on some fancy typewriter. By what computer printer, in what office, by what hand – what I would have done for that bit of card, in the months ahead. A bit o' proof. A bit o' reality. A bit o' evidence.

EDDIE (*speaks*). Got it.

STOKER (*low, with a false half-smile*). Just one thing, whatever you do, when you've picked up the – package. Don't open it, will you?

EDDIE (*low, close to Stoker's face*). Who knows how the spirit will move, old son?

STOKER (*low, also close to him. Stoker is now sweating*). Don't. Just don't. Brother.

11. Exterior. Montage of London cityscapes. Peckham to Kennington. Night.

A blast of music. Eddie speaks over it. He is not seen in the montage. The images of streets, lights, estates, beat-up shops, early evening bus queues, terrace houses with corrugated iron at their doors and windows etc. come again in the episode, but here they are presented pell-mell, heroically, madly, to match Eddie's self-aggrandising state of mind.

EDDIE (*voice over*). Got some dutch courage in me. Drink. Broke into the first twenty Stoker had slipped me, to finance it. Had to, for the evening's madness. Before I set out, I mean what was this? Trail o' mystery addresses, one side o' London to the other? At the best of times when you got to go across town, you've got to have a few to make it, no? Dear – old – London – Town. Funny how you don't ever look at the place where you were born. Less you're doing something a bit unusual. Well, this was unusual. And I looked – South London, what a scaggy dump. What do we all live in this for, I thought – y'know, the way you do when you're out at night, a bit pissed. Let alone a bit – (*A pause.*) Scared shitless.

And cut at once from Eddie's voice
over to:

12. Exterior. Kennington tower block. Night.

*No music. Eddie finds the door,
mumbling the address to himself. There is
a light in the kitchen, the curtains pulled.
He tries, quickly, to peek in. His
movements are hyperactive. He rings the
bell once, at once the lights go out. With
a flourish of his thumb he rings the bell
again. The lights come back on. He
gestures to himself – 'What is this?' He
goes to ring the bell again but before he
can, the door is opened. A thin young
woman. She is pale-faced, blue beneath
her eyes.*

EDDIE. Something to pick up?

13. Interior. Tower block flat. Night.

*Eddie in the doorway. The young woman
walks away from him into the flat,
hunched, her arms folded. He hesitates
for a second then follows, jauntily. She
dodges back round him, slams the door
and leans on it.*

> *Cut at once to:*

14. Flashback to Scene 3. Interior Dana's flat. Night.

A few seconds.
*The fight with his wife Dana; Eddie
caught wrong-footed by her violence.*

> *Cut back to:*

15. Interior. Tower block flat. Night.

EDDIE. Er –

> *Leaning against the front door, the
> young woman points towards the
> kitchen. Eddie turns and looks.*

16. Interior. Tower block flat's kitchen. Night.

*Music. On the draining-board, the parcel
waits. It is in the shape of an old*
fashioned hat-box, covered in the Sun
newspaper, stuck down with aggressive-
looking thick, brown, sticky tape. It looks
sinister. Move around it. Then Eddie
approaches the parcel.

EDDIE (*a gesture to the young woman*).
  Er – ?

> *Nothing from the young woman, who
> still leans against the front door in the
> hallway. He picks the parcel up and
> walks towards her.*

EDDIE. S'cuse me.

YOUNG WOMAN. They –

> *She stares, then opens the front door
> for him.*

EDDIE (*a little slurred*). Thank you.
  Thank you very much.

> *He goes out of the door.*

17. Exterior. Montage of London cityscapes. Night.

*This time, Eddie appears in the montaged
scenes, carrying the parcel. He waits in a
bus queue at Camberwell Green. Then he
is on Waterloo Station. Then on the tube.
Look at faces in the carriage. A woman
moves little parcels in screwed-up
newspaper from one plastic bag to
another. Eddie looks at her and clutches
his parcel protectively.*

EDDIE (*voice over*). Girl in the flat, was
  she stoned? Or just scared o' me?
  Couldn't tell. Na. I flatter myself. Back
  I went into the city. London. City like
  a woman with dirt round the edge of
  her skirt. (*He hiccoughs.*) I thought.

18. Exterior. Houses round Regent's Park West. Night.

*Look at them, gliding past the big houses,
the trees, the old-fashioned lampposts, the
elaborate gates. Faintly, beautiful flute
music.*

EDDIE (*voice over*). Regent's Park. It's
  not just the zoo – it's great big white
  houses. Money, standing there. Piles of
  brick, all painted white, singing o'
  money. You can hear what's inside,
  singing, faintly, on the night air – a
  whole bloody opera of Persian carpets,

silver spoons, crystal decanters, chandeliers, tinklin' away. The money in this country! Where I come from, we do not know the half of it. I remember, in a Peckham pub, some poor old git, holes in the knees of his trousers, scruffy old dog at his feet, saying how for forty years he'd voted Tory – 'cos we're all equal nowadays. They must think we're fools. Mind you, I always voted Tory but then I'm a loyalist to the Queen. That don't mean I wouldn't hang the rich as soon as blink. Anyway. I found the second address.

19. Exterior. House in Regent's Park West. Night.

Eddie tiptoeing along a veranda to the front door. No lights from the house. The windows are shuttered.

EDDIE (*voice over*). No lights. Sort of doors – shutters – behind the windows.

He pulls the bell. He looks about.

(*Aloud. Low.*) What is this? What is this?

(*Voice over.*) Nothing.

(*Speaks:*) Sod this for a load of bananas!

He puts the parcel down outside the door. He turns away but then stops.

(*Voice over.*) Hang about I thought. Someone owes me four hundred quid. Not a *great* thought. But a *clear* thought, on a somewhat unclear evening.

He goes up to the door and picks up the parcel.

Cut at once to:

20. Exterior. The house in Regent's Park West. Night.

The light in one of the rooms is switched on behind Eddie's back. As he turns, the light goes off.

21. Interior. Taxi. Night.

Eddie sitting in a taxi, hatbox on lap.

TAXI DRIVER (*nods at the parcel*). What you got in there?

EDDIE. Four hundred quid.

The taxi-driver shrugs.

22. Exterior. Wasteground, to the side of Vauxhall Bridge on the South Bank. Night.

Eddie goes through the broken fence onto the wasteground. He goes to the river's edge. He kneels, the parcel before him. He takes out a penknife. He slashes at the newspaper. The brown tape is hard to cut. He gets the paper and the tape off, pulling it. An old-fashioned leather hatbox is revealed. He stands. He looks about him. He sees the river. Light pours from the near-by office block throwing the mounds, grass and weeds, dumped prams and rubbish of the wasteground into relief. He looks down at the hatbox. He bends and takes off the lid in one movement. He cannot see into the hatbox. He lifts the hatbox and turns it to the light from the office block.
Inside is a woman's head, the eyes open.
He turns the hatbox in the light.

EDDIE (*voice over*). What was really horrible was I didn't feel a thing. 'Ah,' I said to myself. 'A severed head. Right-ho. Off we go.'

Cut at once to:

23. Exterior. Wasteground, to the side of Vauxhall Bridge on the South Bank. Night.

Same location.
The hatbox a distance away from a crouching Eddie, who is finishing a fit of retching. He stands.

EDDIE (*voice over*). But I couldn't be sick. I stood up. 'Good,' I thought. 'I'm not pissed anymore. Right. What to do?'

24. Exterior. Low-tide river mud, down from the wasteground. Night.

Eddie walks through the river's mud to the water's edge. He wades into the water up to his knees. He sinks the hatbox in the water, with a weary, stooped look to his shoulders. The hatbox lid is under his arm. The box sunk, he flips the lid out onto the stream.

EDDIE (*voice over*). Thought, as I did it, 'Good Old Father Thames'. Fish coming back, in't there? Salmon. See fisherman, off the steps of County Hall. One thing to say for Red Ken – salmon for tea, if you've got a rod and line.

He pauses.

(*Speaks.*) Oh no!

He stands there, helpless.

(*Voice over.*) What if one of Red Ken's fishermen fishes out her head?

(*Speaks.*) No! No!

25. Exterior. The Oval. Bus queue. Night.

Eddie covered in mud. People in the bus queue look at him.

EDDIE (*voice over*). Made it to the Oval. Thought – I have got to get a bus, I am dying. But why was everyone looking at me? Oh the smell! The mud. Father Thames stinks.

Eddie backs away from the bus queue. One old woman in particular is staring at him aggressively.

(*Voice over.*) Leper. Like a leper.

26. Interior. Caractacus's basement room. Night.

It is minimally furnished. A mattress on the floor against the wall. A sleeping-bag against another wall. An electric fire and an electric kettle, the kettle on an old tin tray. Caractacus is in bed on the mattress with a young white woman, Jill. Eddie has just come in through the door. He is still covered in mud.

CARACTACUS. Where you been, boy?

JILL. Hey Caractacus, who is this?

CARACTACUS. This is my white brother. He lives here. (*To Eddie:*) Man, what's the smell?

EDDIE. Jesus, give us a drink.

JILL. What do you mean, he lives here? You just asked *me* to live here.

CARACTACUS. Be cool, it'll all go down, the white man sleeps on the floor.

JILL. We been sleeping on the floor!

CARACTACUS (*leaping out of bed*). What do you want to drink? I got rice tea.

EDDIE. God I can't stop shaking –

JILL. You expect me to move in – sleep on a mattress on the floor, with a few feet away some madman covered in mud?

CARACTACUS. We's all on the sweet planet together. Turning round the sun, all in each other's arms.

JILL (*getting up fast, grabbing her clothes*). You told me you loved me. I fell for it. Me! Born in bloody Peckham! I believed a petty little crook when he told me he loved me! Why? Why? Why do I never learn?

EDDIE. I know what's happenin'! I have been given drugs. By some freak. I have not just thrown a cut-off head into the Thames. I am not standing here covered in mud. Some snotty little dealer off the estates, slipped something in my beer. I'm still here in the pub, in't it! Dribblin' in my beer.

He curls his hand round a non-existent glass, looks down at it.

Oh my God.

Jill and Caractacus are staring at him after his outburst.

CARACTACUS (*very straight*). I have come to a conclusion. We got to be hard to be kind, hard to be kind, hard to be kind. I'm working out each day with some brothers. Be hard to be kind to be *free*, boy. That's why I got nothing in the place but rice tea. That's why I moved in a good woman to live with us.

JILL. What do you mean 'with us'? You two got some kind o' sick idea or something?

The door bursts open. Policemen pour into the room. In a flash they throw everything about.

CARACTACUS. Hey. hey! You's invadin' my privacy –

RED-FACED POLICEMAN. Shut your mouth.

CARACTACUS (*mildly*). Man, I'm jus' working on some kindness here –

The red-faced policeman hits Caractacus in the stomach. He doubles up. Jill open-mouthed with shock. Eddie still with the phantom pint in his hand. The picture – as if frozen. Many men in the wrecked room, standing at dramatic angles. The shade hanging off the light.

EDDIE (*voice over*). I said to myself – all right, relax. I am at the bar of the Lord Castlereagh. This madness – it will go on for a couple o' hours, then the dear old grey world will be back. With a hell of a hangover.

WHITE-FACED POLICEMAN (*plainclothed*). Well. What a number of possibilities we have here.

EDDIE. Think so?

WHITE FACE. Absolutely. I mean – the two of you running her on the game, are you?

JILL. I don't know what you think –

RED FACE (*very close and menacingly to her*). Sh.

WHITE FACE. Then there's all this hi-fi and video gear stacked in the corner.

Eddie glances at the empty corner of the room.

EDDIE. Yeah?

WHITE FACE. To the ceiling son. Do you deny it?

EDDIE. I see what you mean.

WHITE FACE. And were we to rip up the floorboards in here, I bet we would have a good kilo of heroin.

A silence. All dead still.

The biggest international drug-ring conspiracy for years. Broken, utterly.

EDDIE. That would depend on your supplies.

WHITE FACE (*he puts his face very close to Eddie's. He speaks low*). Oh, we are very well supplied.

EDDIE (*low*). I don't think I know you.

WHITE FACE. But I know you.

Very close, look at them, eye to eye.

RED FACE (*leaning over very close to Caractacus*). Suffering are you?

CARACTACUS. I am just taking a rest here.

RED FACE. You are going to need it. End of tonight? Oh dear. Come the dawn you are going to wish you stuck with your own kind. Wish you'd never known your nigger-loving white friend here.

Back to the close-up of Eddie with the white-faced policeman.

EDDIE (*swallows nervously*). What is this? Harrassment?

WHITE FACE. Harrassment? (*He smiles.*) I don't think you know the meaning of the word, old son. Yet.

A pause.

EDDIE. What – coppers are you?

The eye of the white-faced policeman, the eye of the red-faced policeman.

From what manor?

A pause.

Who? What? Are you?

WHITE FACE (*close – then suddenly he hits Eddie in the face. Shouts –*). Get 'em out! Get 'em out!

27. Exterior. Street. Night.

Outside Caractacus's basement flat. Three cars. Two are police cars, lights flashing. The other is a large black car, the window-glass dark. Caractacus and Jill, struggling, are being carried to the police cars. Eddie glances at them as he is forced toward the big black car.

Shouting. Flashing lights. Kicking and struggling bodies – this mayhem very briefly, contrasting with –

Cut at once to:

28. Interior. Moving car. Night.

Calm. The car's engine barely audible. Eddie is sitting in the back, handcuffed, next to a heavy-set middle-aged man, Eldridge, who wears a fine suit and coat.

The car is driven by a chauffeur. Next to the chauffeur sits a young man with an immaculate, beautifully groomed head of blonde hair. The fine wool of his coat and collar exude class and wealth. As the car drives, Eddie looks down the side of the young man's head. He sees he is wearing a small gold ear-ring in his right ear. The young man, not revealed in this scene, is Hugo Silver.
The drive. Silence. Through the window, night-time South London. Eldridge, looking out of the window.

ELDRIDGE (*upper-class voice*). 'Human kind cannot bear very much reality.'

EDDIE. Sorry?

ELDRIDGE. A line by T.S. Eliot.

EDDIE. ?

ELDRIDGE. A twentieth-century poet. Probably the worst line he ever wrote.

EDDIE (*voice over*). There was a smell about 'em. I thought – they are wearing scent! But lookin' back – it was probably just heavy Old Spice. But at the time I thought – scent? Quoting bleeding poetry? Jesus H. Christ, had I been – what? Set up, kidnapped, by higher ranks of gay police officers? I did not fancy the night ahead, one little bit.

ELDRIDGE (*still looking out of the window*). In your nasty little way, Eddie, you think you are tough. Even a little cruel. But you have no idea how the world is run. How toughly, how cruelly. You have no choice but to go the way we want you to go.

EDDIE. What are you talkin' about?

Eldridge hands Eddie a photograph. It is of the hatbox, opened, well-photographed, the woman's head staring up.

EDDIE (*voice over*). And I went. I am ashamed to say. I – pissed my trousers.

Without comment Eldridge presses a button. The window next to him motors down. Wind in the car.

EDDIE (*aloud. Shouts*). Nothing to do wi' me! All I know is – I am owed four hundred quid for this little lot!

Nothing from the men in the car.

What have you to do with all this?

Nothing from the men.

That house in Regent's Park, that you?

Nothing from the men.

What are you lot? Stinkin' o' scent?

ELDRIDGE. We have our smell. You, I see, have yours.

Eddie moves his handcuffed hands to hit him. And Eldridge has a pistol in his hand, as if from nowhere. He speaks calmly to the driver.

Here.

The car pulls up. Eldridge, suddenly military.

Put your hands out!

Mesmerised, Eddie raises his hands. Eldridge undoes the handcuffs, still holding the gun. Then, very sveltly he says –

Now. How can I put this in a way that you will understand?

Suddenly Hugo Silver roars with laughter. Eddie stares at the back of his head. For the first time, Eldridge is disconcerted.

Let me put it like this –

From Eldridge, a look of daggers at the back of Silver's head.
Eldridge speaks, mute, to Eddie. Eddie's voice over, over his mouthings –

EDDIE (*voice over*). It was that laugh. The way the fat sod looked at the neck of the other one – that did it for me. I went cold. With hate. The first time in my life. I mean, I've hated, who has not? But always, I dunno hotly – not cold. Cold as ice. That laugh, that look –

Cut at once to:

29. Flashback of Scene 28. Interior. Car. Night.

A flash – repeat of the moment when Silver laughs and Eldridge looks at the back of his head.

Cut back to:

30. Interior. Car. Night.

EDDIE (*voice over*). It was – weak. That's what made me hate 'em. The dead cold flash of the thought – maybe I can defeat these pissers. Turn round on whatever it was they were doin' to me –

ELDRIDGE. Have you heard one word I have said to you?

EDDIE (*weakly*). Sorry, I –

ELDRIDGE (*sighs. Then deadly*). There is something called the sword of Damocles.

EDDIE. Oh yeah?

ELDRIDGE. Look on it as an atomic bomb, in a satellite, circling forever round your head. Which, at the press of a button, can blast you into dust. Just you, Eddie. Your personal atom bomb. That is what the unusual events of this evening mean to you.

EDDIE. Fate.

ELDRIDGE (*surprised*). Why yes. Now. This girl you so horribly murdered.

EDDIE. What –

ELDRIDGE. I mean, the thing with the head was bad enough but you should have seen what you did to the body.

Look very close at Eddie's face and at Eldridge's mouth.

EDDIE. What –

ELDRIDGE. Your finger dabs, all over the hatbox.

EDDIE. What – ah – I threw it in the water.

ELDRIDGE. And the hatbox. Belongs to your ex-wife.

EDDIE. Does it?

ELDRIDGE. Oh yes! Your Dana has become a high-flyer. Fur coats. Silk dresses. Lovely hats – in leather boxes. As I see it, you burgled her place.

EDDIE (*hysterical*). Yeah yeah why not? S'pose you got my dabs all over, too –

ELDRIDGE. What you have got to get into your mind, is that your own little, Third World War nuclear explosion is personally arranged. Your bomb can go off any time. But don't worry, like the real thing, it may never happen.

EDDIE. Oh. Good.

ELDRIDGE. So.

He leans over and opens the door next to Eddie. Who sits still.

Go and live your life, Eddie. Back into the night.

A smile.

Here's a thousand quid for expenses.

He tosses an envelope into Eddie's lap.

And as a gesture of goodwill –

He produces a bottle of whisky.

Glenmorangie. The best. Duty-free size. You deserve it. Off you go.

Eddie still sitting there, mouth open.

Don't shoot your mouth off too much. I mean, what will you say? I threw a severed head into the Thames and was given a thousand pounds by the Special Branch, who smelt of scent? Oh, and – my regards to Dana.

EDDIE (*he stares at the back of Hugo Silver's head in the front seat*). Why me? Why me? Why me?

Eddie grabs the sides of Silver's head and tries to turn it. Eldridge hits Eddie on the side of the neck with his gun.
Show the gun from Eddie's view, coming toward him.
The screen kaleidoscopes into pain.

31. Exterior. Derelict site. Dawn.

Seen from above, Eddie wakes. Then stands very quickly, whirling about, slipping on rubble and rubbish. He rages at the derelict ground. This with a loud blast of music.
Then silence. Eddie dead still. A wino is looking at him. Then come to normal sounds of the city, traffic, birdsong.
The whisky bottle. The wino shuffles towards it. Eddie pushes him away, picks up the whisky bottle and hugs it. Half-crouching, Eddie and the wino glare at each other. Eddie slashes out a foot, the wino retreats. Eddie finds the packet of money and opens it.

EDDIE (*voice over*). A bottle o' the best whisky in the world. Fifty twenty-quid notes with Her Majesty's dear face looking up at me. Powerful objects out o' the real world. 'Oh no,' I thought. 'It really happened'.

32. Exterior. Caractacus's basement doorway. Day.

Eddie hammering on the door.

EDDIE (*voice over*). I had to get back home. Where was home? Caractacus's floor. Life out of an Addis sports bag. But I was shattered. Been hit twice in the head. And a night out in the city, under the stars, sounds romantic. Your shirt goes like corrugated iron, cutting your armpits. Also I was developing a heavy fear of open spaces.

He gives up hammering. He tries the doorknob. The door swings open. He hesitates then goes in.

33. Interior. Caractacus's flat. Day.

The floor is full of Jamaicans, asleep, all men, with sleeping-bags.

EDDIE. Hey! Wakey wakey!

One sleeper, who is at Eddie's feet, turns over and looks up.

Where's Caractacus?

SLEEPER. Who wants to know?

EDDIE. Don't give me that! Don't give me bloody that!

He kicks the sleeper.

Hey!

And at once all the sleepers in the room rise, confronting Eddie.

Yeah. Well. I – just dropped by for my bag. S'cuse me.

He walks between the standing figures. He picks up a bag, turns; with a big false grin, he makes for the door. The sleeper stops him with a finger on his chest.

SLEEPER. You Eddie?

EDDIE (*looks over his shoulder*). Maybe.

SLEEPER. Letter for you.

He hands Eddie a letter.

EDDIE. Oh. Ta.

34. Exterior. Outside Caractacus's basement flat. Day.

Eddie leans against the wall, exhausted. He opens the letter.

35. Exterior. Outside Caractacus's basement flat. Day.

Same location.
   Close up of the letter.

   It reads:

   Be hard.
   To be kind.
   Go well.
   C.

EDDIE (*voice over*). What is this? I thought. Betrayal?

36. Exterior. Tower block landing. Day.

The tower block where he picked up the parcel. Eddie blundering along the landing.

EDDIE (*voice over*). I'd gone right through being tired, out the other side of knackerdom. I blundered round the city, scenes of last night's nightmare. Trouble was, though it was a lovely sunny morning, the nightmare got worse.

He finds the door. It is boarded-up with plywood. There is a big aerosoled graffito on it – the anarchist symbol, a circle round a capital 'A'.

37. Exterior. Outside the house in Regent's Park West. Day.

Eddie lurches off a bus. He stands across the street looking at the house. A policeman is standing at the front door. Eddie lurches across the road clutching the bottle of whisky. The policeman stares at him, Eddie turns away.

   Wipe to:

38. Exterior. Vauxhall Bridge. Day.

Eddie at the side of the bridge looking down onto the wasteground and the river.

Seen from below, the bridge. Eddie swigs from the whisky bottle.

   Wipe to:

39. Exterior. The pub. Day.

The pub where Eddie met Stoker. Eddie is walking up and down. He is in a filthy temper. He passes the door now and then, kicking it. He swigs from the whisky bottle. The publican looks through the glass then opens the door. Eddie pushes his way in. Sound – traffic.

   Wipe to:

40. Interior. The pub. Day.

Same location. A few minutes later. Eddie being thrown out of the pub. The publican gesturing at him to go away.

EDDIE. What do you mean, 'barred'?

PUBLICAN. You are barred from this pub.

EDDIE. But you know me –

PUBLICAN. Bloody winos, bloody fantasists –

EDDIE. It's Stoker I want, Stoker –

   The publican slams the door and locks it. Eddie takes another, though half-hearted kick at the door.

(*Voice over.*) In twenty-four hours, how far can you go down?

41-45. A collage of South London derelict sites, streets etc. Day.

Over it Eddie speaking.

EDDIE (*voice over*). South London. The foxes are doing well. Out the dustbins. Better than the bloody humans. All day I stumbled around. Drinking their scotch. Well! They wanted me to, didn't they? Drink their scotch, spend their money. OK! OK! Off I went. In a nose dive. My brain in rags, yeah, my brains pulled out o' my head, waving like flags over the crummy houses, the traffic, the dirty dogshit grass.

   Over:

42. Graffiti-covered bridge.

Over a broad railway embankment Eddie stands and looks. No trains come. He turns. A fox stands on the bridge, looking at him. The fox turns and saunters away.

43. Before the gates of a garage yard.

Cars up on bricks in the street. Alsation dogs jumping up at Eddie as he staggers past the gates.

44. Second-hand junk shop.

The shop's wares are piled up outside on the pavement – broken, stained furniture, gas stoves, old mangles, irons, piles of worn out kettles, pots, pans. Eddie stumbles into the junk. A woman in a white shop-coat and crumpled apron comes out of the shop and shoos him away, angrily.

45. Traffic island.

Eddie on the island, spinning, the traffic passing him.

46. Exterior. Camberwell Green. Early evening.

Top shot.
   Eddie is asleep in the centre of the Green, on a bench. Traffic circles the Green, seen through trees and bushes.

EDDIE (*voice over*). Woke up. Head crystal clear. Rush o' thoughts. O' taking on the whole bloody world. Only trouble was I couldn't stand up.

   Eddie trying to swing his legs off the bench and stand. He can't make it. Other down-and-out men and women are looking at him. He panics – realises he is still clutching the whisky bottle and his bag. He searches for the packet of money, finds it.

Then I saw where I was. Camberwell Green. My wife's flat! Just over the way! Peabody Buildings! I flooded myself with superhuman will.

Eddie stands elaborately, steps forward, steps back, steadies himself. Catch one malevolent look from a down-and-out man. Eddie looks away across the Green. On the pavement side of the railings, partly obscured by a bush, a large young man in a raincoat, standing legs apart, hands in pockets, is watching him. Eddie looks away, then glances back after a moment. The large young man is no longer there.

47. Interior. Stairway, Peabody Buildings. Early evening.

Eddie lurches up the stairway. He leans against the wall as a young couple carry a child in a push-chair down the stairs, with great care.

48. Interior. Stairway, Peabody Buildings. Early evening.

Outside his wife's door. He is pulling clothes about in his bag. He finds a key, puts it in the keyhole.

49. Interior. Dana's flat. Early evening.

It is expensively and elaborately furnished, drapes, beautiful furniture, soft sofa and armchairs, standard lamps. Eddie runs into the living-room. She is wearing a full-length silk dress.

EDDIE. What is all this, Dana?

DANA. Get out, Eddie.

EDDIE. All this gear, what is it –

He falls over.

DANA. You dirt –

She kicks him in the side.

Cut at once to:

50. Interior. Dana's flat: bedroom. Early evening.

Eddie is carrying a struggling Dana by the waist into the bedroom. More luxury. He throws her on the bed.

EDDIE. What you been doing, you bitch?

Cut at once to:

51. Interior. Dana's flat: bedroom. Early evening.

Same location. A few minutes later. Eddie is pulling expensive dresses, coats, furs from out of a fitted cupboard. He comes across a suit and some shirts. He pauses, exhausted. He turns. Dana is smoking a cigarette, calmly.

EDDIE. What d'you do for fancy hats, then?

Nothing from Dana. She looks at him cooly.

Right! I'm moving back in!

Cut at once to:

52. Interior. Dana's flat: bathroom. Early evening.

Eddie in the bath. His clothes are on the floor. The bottle of whisky at his lips. He looks at the end of the bath. There is a full range of men's Old Spice. Look at it. There is a shaving mug, shaving brush and razor. He picks up the razor.

EDDIE (*low*). Bloody hell.

Dana comes into the bathroom. She carries a silk, Japanese-style dressing-gown over her shoulder and a large kitchen-knife, which she dangles from finger and thumb. He sees the knife. He whirls in the water in panic, raising the whisky bottle as a weapon.

DANA (*she laughs, gaily*). Relax. I'm making you some dinner. Liver do you?

EDDIE. Oh. Yeah. Ta love –

DANA. Put this on. (*She tosses the dressing-gown onto his clothes.*) You look bloody awful already. You may as well look bloody ridiculous as well.

She turns to go.

EDDIE (*pointing at the Old Spice*). Whose is all this poncy stuff, then?

DANA. Who's asking?

EDDIE. Your bloody husband.

DANA. Really? I thought he was dead.

EDDIE (*voice over*). My loving wife. Still the same. All come, all go.

He picks up a tin of Old Spice talcum powder. He drops it into the bath water.

53. Interior. Dana's flat: bathroom. Early evening.

Same location. A few minutes later.
Eddie is wearing the dressing-gown. He has put all the Old Spice things into the sink and is running hot water over them. He is shaving in the mirror, humming 'All you need is love'.

54. Interior. Dana's flat: bedroom. Night.

Eddie and Dana are in bed, making love. Very close to them, shots gliding into each other.

EDDIE (*voice over*). There was something coming off her, off her skin – like she was older, but younger. Something silky. Something – learnt. I mean, I pride myself when it comes to a turnover with a chick. But this, I don't know. Dana and I, we'd been fifteen rounds together, one way and another. I broke her arm once, for which she had her revenge – nearly had my right eye out a month later. Yeah we knew each other very well. But this was a stranger, who'd been swimming in strange waters. Bathing in milk and honey. It was frightening, something deep, like you know someone's got blue eyes, you've stared into 'em many a time. You meet a year later in bed –and her eyes have turned green.

55. Interior. Dana's flat: bedroom. Night.

Same location. Later.
Dana is smoking.

EDDIE. You think I'm lying through my teeth.

Dana says nothing.

You think I've been on the piss and that's that.

A pause.

Well! Well! (*Really miserable.*) It's good to be loved. And believed.

DANA. Don't cry Eddie. Last time you cried you threw an electric fire at me.

She looks at a bedside table to stub out her cigarette. He grabs her wrist.

EDDIE. Who are they Dana, love?! He, they – put this stuff in this flat! Walked off with your hatbox!

DANA. Haven't got an hatbox! Only Princess Margaret, Princess Di have hatboxes, royalty! You should know, being so keen on 'em.

EDDIE (*letting her wrist go*). I could say – (*Exhausted.*) Say we – (*Yawning.*) We deserve each other. (*He closes his eyes.*)

DANA (*getting up, stubbing the cigarette out*). I don't think so. You're like death warmed up. Have a sleep.

EDDIE. What – warmed – ?

He's asleep.

56. A dream.

The fox on the graffiti-covered bridge, as in Scene 42. Eddie turns and sees the fox. The light is speckled with blue. Eddie looking; he blinks. He sees Dana crouching before him, instead of the fox. She stands and saunters away.

57. Interior. Dana's flat: bedroom. Night.

Eddie wakes up in the bed. He looks around sharply, is still for a second, then –

EDDIE (*jumping out of bed*). Bitch!

Naked, he runs into the living-room, follow him – the camera hand-held. Dana has a telephone in her hand. She looks at him. Calmly she puts the telephone down.

Bitch!

He grabs the telephone and pulls the wire out.

DANA. They'll be round in twenty minutes.

EDDIE. You smell of 'em. The cream puffs in the car.

DANA. Twenty minutes, Eddie.

EDDIE. What are you, their whore?

DANA (*deadly*). You wanna break my arm? You wanna cut my head off, put it in my hatbox?

Eddie runs out of the room. Follow him to:

58. Interior. Dana's flat: bedroom. Night.

Eddie runs into the bedroom. He flings the fitted cupboard open and pulls at the man's clothing.

Cut at once to:

59. Interior. Dana's flat: bedroom. Night.

A few minutes later.
   Eddie, dressed in the suit. It is too long for him. He stuffs other clothes into his sports bag. He whirls around the room. This to a hand-held camera. He sees a small cupboard. He pulls it. It's locked. He kicks it hard. It splinters. He pulls the door off. He reaches inside and finds a hatbox in his hands. He looks at it, terrified. He opens it. Inside – is a big, Ascot-like floppy hat, covered in cherries.

Cut at once to:

60. Interior. Dana's flat: living-room. Night.

Eddie, running into the living-room. He confronts Dana who is standing in the same place. He throws the hat at her. It skims through the air like a frisbee. Elegantly she catches it then, with a toss of her head, flips her hair back and puts the hat on. She looks at him – the hat and the silk dress. She looks like an aristocrat at Ascot.

EDDIE. OK. OK. OK.

61. Exterior. Outside the Peabody Buildings. Night.

A blast of music, very loud, as Eddie runs from the stairway. He runs across the asphalt. He rests, panting. He looks out across the shadow. A car has pulled up. Four big men in baseball jackets are rushing out of the car, leaving the doors open, and up the stairway. A driver sits at the wheel. Eddie steps back.

EDDIE (*voice over*). Big guys. 'Filth' written all over 'em. I stepped back in the shadows. That is a talent I do have.

62. Exterior. Newsagent's window. Day.

Eddie is looking at cards in the window.

EDDIE (*voice over*). One thousand pound. Actually, not much. I found a room.

A card in the window reads: '£35 pw' written in biro.

63. Interior. Eddie's room. Day.

It is small. The wallpaper is bright yellow and green stripes. The carpet is mauve and red. There is a single bed; a large wardrobe; no chair; a wash basin. A silent Pakistani woman is taking money from Eddie.

EDDIE (*voice over*). In a fit o' being my own Chancellor o' the Exchequer I paid three months ahead.

64. Interior. Eddie's room.

Same location. Some days later.
   Eddie lies on the bed in a bad way, drinking. Look at him from above.

EDDIE (*voice over. NB; the scenes to glide, wipe into each other under his commentary*). It was a real wank pit. But I needed time. Shed my old skin, put on a new one.

65. A collage. Flashbacks.

The images folding quickly one into the other, in the speckled blue colour of the previous dream sequence – the boarded tower block door – Caractacus's flat, the Jamaican men going up and down the staircase – the house in Regent's Park, a policeman still outside.

EDDIE (*voice over*). A week or so, I kept going back to where it had happened. I felt like a ghost. Looking for some kind of sign from the living that I was there. But nothing.

66. Exterior. Peabody Buildings – outside Dana's flat. Day.

The four heavy men are moving the

furniture from the flat out onto the asphalt.

EDDIE (*voice over*). Dana moved out. There was no sign of her. Whatever crazy people my once-beloved was mixed up with, they sure looked after their property.

67. Interior. Eddie's room. Night.

Eddie is washing his face in the basin. Pound notes are spread out on the bed.

EDDIE (*voice over*). Then I gave up hanging around. The weeks – and the cash – went. And I pulled myself together.

68. Interior. Eddie's room. Night.

Same location. Later.
  Eddie, doing press ups, then running on the spot, in his underpants.

EDDIE (*voice over*). Sod it, I thought! They will not get me! I began to use that hate. I could begin to feel – a new skin, growin' over me. Then, one day:

69. Exterior. Street. Day.

Eddie at a distance, among passers-by, buying an Evening Standard; *then – close to him. The front of the newspaper has a headline: 'THAMES HEAD HORROR' and a picture of Vauxhall Bridge. Eddie, reading it. He rips through the paper to find more.*

EDDIE (*shouts*). Bastards!

Some passers-by look at him.

(*To the startled paper-seller:*) The H-bomb's gone off!

NEWSPAPER-SELLER. Well, that's the racing page for you, old son.

EDDIE. What! Yeah. Yeah.

70. Exterior. Crowded street. Day.

Eddie turns and runs, throwing the paper away. He disappears into the people in the street.

EDDIE (*voice over*). So. It started. A right season in hell.

End of Episode 1.

Over the credits a screaming, heavy-metal rendering of the children's nursery rhyme:

Pussycat, pussycat
Where have you been?
I've been to London
To see the Queen.

Pussycat, pussycat
What did you there?
I frightened a mouse
Under her chair.

Episode 2

Anything for England

Episode 2

Characters

EDDIE CASS	Denis Lawson
HUGO SILVER	Simon Callow
ELDRIDGE	George Baker
DANA	Lindsay Duncan
CLIVE	James Warwick
SANDRA	Tacy Kneale
MRS EPWORTH	Ellen Sheean
WILLIAMS	Gabriel Connaughton
OLD MAN	Mischa de la Motte
MAN IN LOVE	Colin Meredich
MEN IN COUNTRY PUB	John Baxter
	Norman Cooley
	Nicholas Hutchison
	Richard Huw
LADIES IN COUNTRY PUB	Faith Kent
	Meriel Scholfield
	Barbara Wilshire
STUNT ARRANGER	Gareth Milne

i EDDIE: 'Are you telling me, all the crap that's happened to me – the people behind it are MI5?'

ii HUGO: 'You have no idea who I am, where I come from?'

iii EDDIE: 'Where was I? On another planet?'

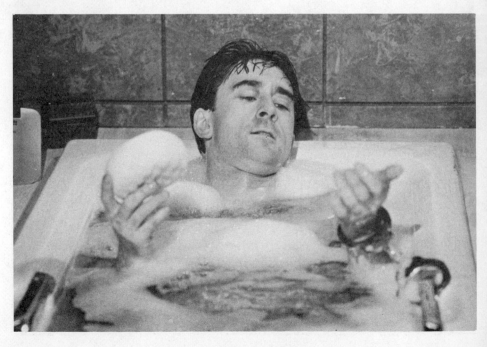

iv ELDRIDGE in the war room.

v HUGO: 'I know a pub nearby.'

vi DANA: 'They know what you're doing all the time. You can't ever win, Eddie.'

vii EDDIE: 'He killed someone . . . Who is he?'

1. Reprise. Flashbacks.

A kaleidoscope of images, mute, from the first episode, to Eddie's commentary.

EDDIE (*voice over*). So who's runnin' the world then? Who's sayin' do this, do that?

Who's pissing you about?

Who's pulling the puppet strings?

How life is to be lived, eh? Bloody hell, when the world goes mad, what you got to be? A bloody philosopher?

All I knew was –

Show Eddie reading the Standard *headline, shouting and running.*

My own private atom bomb had gone off, right over my head.

2. Blank screen.

EDDIE (*voice over*). First thing I did was to rob my landlady.

3. Interior. Eddie's room. Early evening.

Eddie nudging the Pakistani woman on the arm. She hands him a five-pound note from a bankroll with each nudge. Look at this from above.

EDDIE (*voice over*). God, or the gods, forgive me. But my only weapons I reckoned were cash, luck, anger. The greatest of these was cash.

4. Exterior. Euston Station. Twilight.

The station as a nightmare vision. Under the arches of the approach to the station – where taxis draw up – football supporters scuffle and vomit. Eddie walks through them.
  A blast of music, deep, descending chords of brass.
  A police constable stumbles back out of the mêlée of football supporters, clutching his crotch. Eddie passes him.

5. Interior. Train: buffet. Night.

All men, heavy-drinking; the men all fat

and ashen-faced, jabbering away. Eddie sits at the table nursing a can. The table crowded with cans, paper cups, bits of pork pie. The air thick with smoke. The carriage lurches, the drinkers sway.*

EDDIE (*voice over*). Got on a train thinking – where do I hide? Thought, 'Right. Countryside. No one about. Sleep in barns. Walk along hedges. Be a tramp. Eat bloody nuts 'n' berries.' I thought. Out o' my skull, with panic 'n' fear.

Eddie suddenly catches the eye of one of the drinkers in the buffet. He has cold eyes, a can in his hand – but he is not drunk. The big lad realises he has been spotted. He turns away at once. Eddie launches after him.

Oi you, you bastard!

(*Voice over, as he rushes after him:*) Was the whole bloody country a goldfish bowl, me wriggling about among the reeds, blue-eyed bastards knockin' on the glass?

DRINKERS (*unexpectedly mild in their reactions*). Oi, steady! Watch it mate! 'Ave a thought for other people! Fair do's!

6. Interior. Train corridor. Night.

Eddie runs along the corridor after the big lad, who suddenly turns on Eddie. Eddie stops, dead still, then begins to back away. But the big lad gestures to him. Eddie hesitates – the big lad gestures again. He walks away quickly. Eddie follows.
  An odd, scuttling scene, the corridor lurching.

7. Interior. Train: first-class carriage. Night.

The carriage is brilliantly lit. The orange seats and the white head-rests hurt the eyes. It is empty. The big lad stands at the end of the carriage, beckoning to Eddie. The camera, from Eddie's view, moves towards him.
  Eddie finds Hugo Silver sitting by the window. Hugo looks up and smiles. Eddie sees the ear-ring in Hugo's earlobe.

8. Flashback insert from Episode 1, Scene 28.

Eddie in the back of the car, looking at the back of Hugo's head. The ear-ring.

EDDIE (*voice over*). The one who sat in the front of the car. When they picked me up. One of 'em. The one who laughed!

Cut to Hugo, laughing, throwing his head back.

Cut at once back to:

9. Interior. Train: first-class carriage. Night.

HUGO (*to the big lad*). Williams. Sit further back would you?

The big lad hesitates.

Oh don't be a bloody idiot.

The big lad squeezes past Eddie, their faces close to each other. Williams goes and sits several seats back down the carriage.

EDDIE (*still in a state of shock*). You're wearin' a bloody ear-ring.

HUGO. Yes. Once, for professional reasons, I had to join a rather nasty little gay scene. In Moscow, actually.

A flash of bad temper.

For Christ's sake sit down.

Eddie hesitates.

Cut at once to:

10. Flashback insert from Episode 1, Scene 30.

Eddie trying to turn Hugo's head – then the gun being rammed in his face – this flashback very quick.

Cut back at once to:

11. Interior. Train: first-class carriage. Night.

HUGO (*looking into the dark beyond the window; low*). Do as you're told, man. If you do not do as you're told you will not believe what will happen to you.

EDDIE. Oh really?

Hugo stares.
Eddie sits down. A silence.

HUGO (*still looking out of the window*). Right. We move. Keep your mouth shut.

He waits a few seconds, then stands and walks down the carriage. Eddie follows, haltingly. The big lad half-stands.

We're going to the buffet, Williams.

Hugo and Eddie leave the carriage, Williams behind them, half-standing, uncertain, looking at them.

12. Interior. Train: corridor. Night.

HUGO. Now!

Hugo and Eddie run down the corridor. At the end of it, Hugo opens the toilet door. Eddie runs into him.

In!

EDDIE. Oi, I –

Hugo pulls Eddie into the toilet.

13. Interior. Train: toilet. Night.

Eddie and Hugo, cramped in the small toilet, the train lurching. Eddie having difficulty keeping his balance.
Their dialogue overlaps.

EDDIE. Don't you, don't you put your hands on me –

HUGO. Listen to me you fool –

EDDIE. I tell you I am no pooftah, I don't know what's happening to me but that's not going t' –

HUGO. You have no idea what is being done to you, you have no idea what for, no idea – (*Not overlapped:*) How bad it is! How dangerous!

EDDIE. OK! OK! Tell me then, 'flower'.

HUGO. First we've got to get away from him.

EDDIE. Who?

HUGO. Williams. My nurse maid.

EDDIE (*shouts*). Who are you? What are you?

HUGO. Just understand! You are a liability. A nothing. There are men in rooms making jokes about you. Playing with you. Deciding how to screw you. All you can do is – do what I say.

Hugo pushes his face to the small patch of clear glass on the lavatory's frosted window.

Dark as hell. We must be near there. (*Turns to Eddie.*) When I say 'go', p ıll your feet up to your chest.

EDDIE. What?

HUGO. Right!

Hugo wrenches the door open.

14. Interior. Train: corridor. Night.

By the toilet door. Williams is standing there, apelike. Hugo runs straight into him. They wrestle.

HUGO (*shouts to Eddie*). Cord!

EDDIE. Sorry?

HUGO. Pull the cord!

Hugo gives the big lad a horrible blow with the edge of his hand, in the face. The big lad slumps back with a grunt. Eddie stares. Then looks to one side – two children, both holding soft toy dolls, are watching.
Hugo, his nose bloody, pulls the communication cord. He struggles with the window, pulls it down, opens the door from outside. The train begins to brake.

Go!

EDDIE (*being pulled by Hugo by the hand toward the door*). No! No! No thanks –

15. Exterior. In mid-air. Night.

A flash of Eddie, turning over and over, holding his knees in mid-air.

EDDIE (*voice over*). My life flashed before me. It did not seem a good idea.

Eddie, screaming.

16. Screen goes dark.

EDDIE (*voice over*). A smell like someone had done a poop.

17. Exterior. Fence, a field beyond. Night.

Hazy at first, then Eddie realises he is looking straight into the calm face of a cow.

EDDIE. Moo cow.

(*Then, voice over:*) Then I remembered. I hate the countryside.

Scuttling, slipping on the embankment, Hugo approaches. Look at him from Eddie's point of view – a thin, bent-over figure, a gangly young man.

HUGO. Spot on. We go.

EDDIE. My back's broken –

HUGO. Rubbish. Play the Englishman.

18. Exterior. Field. Moonlight. Night.

A blast of music – brass, descending chords. Bent over, running, Hugo and Eddie run across a field. Cows lumber away from them.

19. Exterior. Field. Moonlight. Night.

Same location.
Close to them. Eddie stops, then plumps down. Hugo stops and runs back.

HUGO. Get up.

EDDIE (*childish*). Won't. Not going on. Won't play.

A flash of handcuffs.

EDDIE. Ey!

Hugo handcuffs Eddie to him.

Ey! Ey!

HUGO. Now we are married. I think we deserve each other.

Close to Eddie.

EDDIE (*low*). I've – sat on a cow pat.

20. Exterior. Small wood. Early day.

Bushes rustle.

EDDIE (*his voice from the bushes*). I am dying. I know I am dying.

The camera goes into the bushes and discovers Eddie and Hugo, crouched. Eddie is shivering. He looks terrible. Hugo is peeling the paper from a bar of chocolate – Eddie holds his handcuffed hand up obediently.

I hate nature. I've hated nature since I was a kid. Think nature hates me and all.

HUGO. Chocolate. Get your blood sugar up.

EDDIE. Bloody cold, bloody wet, bloody socks like squidgy mud, your underpants all sticky, smellin' o' cowshit. Nature? It's a killer.

HUGO. Survival. Toughen up. (*He scoffs.*) The most wanted man in Britain. Look at you.

EDDIE. Wanted? Don't want to be wanted. Who wants me? What am I doin' here sitting in the middle of a bush, handcuffed to Little Lord Fauntleroy –

Hugo holds up the chocolate. Eddie stares at it, then grabs it and eats. Hugo, looking out.

HUGO. Sanctuary.

21. Exterior. Eighteenth-century farmhouse and surrounding countryside. Early day.

Hugo and Eddie are looking at the lush countryside, the early sun throwing long shadows, mist clearing. A big farmhouse, covered in ivy. The windows glint. The camera roams over the scene which, with the fore-shortening, looks like a painting.

EDDIE (*voice over*). What a pile.

HUGO (*voice over*). The house belongs to a friend of mine. He's away on business. In Japan. I'm sure he won't mind if we put ourselves up for a few days. He only uses the place for the odd weekend. Parties for Nippo businessmen, with a few girls brought in from Birmingham.

EDDIE (*voice over*). Disgustin'.

HUGO (*voice over*). How the other half lives, Eddie. This is the real England, this is the heartland, this is where the power is.

22. Exterior. Farmhouse. Early day.

A back-door. Look down on Eddie and Hugo. Hugo is breaking and entering with great skill, using a wire with clips at each end to by-pass an alarm system.

EDDIE (*voice over; hysterical edge in his voice*). I'll give you this. You'd make a good villain.

HUGO (*voice over*). But I am. I am a very good villain indeed.

23. Interior. Farmhouse. Early day.

A collage of the rooms. They are luxurious with old-fashioned winged chairs, fine curtains, big lampshades, bookshelves, cut glass etc. Beautiful bedrooms, four-poster beds, furry carpets and rugs. Light floral curtains; on some of the pillows fluffy soft toys. Hugo and Eddie burst into each room. Hugo pulls him into each room. Eddie gapes, Hugo pulls him out and slams the doors. Hugo is wild – Eddie is bewildered by his manner.

HUGO (*voice over*). See what you're up against Eddie. You little runt. Get it into your mean, whingeing little soul –

EDDIE (*voice over*). Oh yeah?

HUGO (*voice over*). Silk sheets at night, sunlight in the early morning. The carpets! Your toes curled in lovely rugs, Eddie –

EDDIE (*voice over*). Eh –

HUGO (*voice over*). Sensuality of it, the luxury, they kill for it Eddie –

EDDIE (*voice over*). Hang about –

HUGO (*voice over*). Think you've got a hope against this lot, Eddie? You don't –

EDDIE (*voice over*). Hang about! Slow down!

HUGO (*voice over*). You're a bloody fool Eddie! A bloody little fool!

24. Interior. Farmhouse: bathroom. Day.

Eddie stares at its luxury. This scene not
voice over.

HUGO. Give me your trousers.

EDDIE. Yeah?

HUGO. There's a machine in the scullery.
I'll run them through.

EDDIE. Oh. Thanks.

HUGO. The hot water's instant.

EDDIE (*a slight pause*). Oh. Good. Er –

*He pulls at his trousers, Hugo making
no move to take the handcuffs off.*

25. Interior. Farmhouse: bathroom. Day.

*Eddie lies in the bath. Suds and steam.
He is handcuffed to one of the taps. He
lies still, his arm awkwardly held up
because of his handcuffed hand.*

EDDIE (*voice over*). Where was I, on
another planet? Yeah. I'd been
snatched by a flying saucer. The guy
with the ear-ring was some kind o'
Martian. They'd done something to my
brain, to make me think I was
somewhere where I was not.

*Eddie panics, he splashes about
sloshing water. He shouts.*

(*Aloud:*) What am I doing here? What
am I doing here?

Cut at once to:

26. Interior. Farmhouse: bathroom. Day.

*Same location.
    Hugo is in the bathroom, holding out a
big towel robe to Eddie, without comment.
Eddie pulls at the handcuff. Hugo stares
at him.*

27. Interior. Farmhouse: kitchen. Day.

*Eddie in his robe, sitting facing Hugo
over a long table. A whisky bottle and
fine, cut-glass tumblers before them.
Eddie is handcuffed to the top of the
table-leg. It makes him lean forward
awkwardly. Hugo sips whisky, looking
at him.*

*A pause.
    Then Hugo takes the handcuff key out
of his pocket and skims it along the table
to Eddie. Eddie fumbles with the key and
releases himself, Hugo watching.
    Eddie reaches for the whisky, gulps
some down.*

EDDIE. All right. Who the bloody hell
are you?

HUGO (*staring into his glass*). My father
was a colonel in British Army
Intelligence.

28. Photograph.

*A photograph of a man in Army uniform
flits onto the screen, then disappears.*

29. Interior. Farmhouse: kitchen. Day.

*Hugo's face, close to, staring into his
glass. Look at Eddie's worried face, close
to, then back to Hugo.*

HUGO. I never knew the bastard. When I
was three months in my mother's
womb, he was wounded in Cyprus.

30. Photograph.

*Of a bomb explosion in a Cypriot street.
It fades.*

31. Interior. Farmhouse: kitchen. Day.

Hugo's face.

HUGO. He died of his wounds, the day
after I was born.

He pauses.

England, oh happy England.

32. Photograph.

*A DSO medal in a case. Pull back. It is
surrounded by photographs of Hugo's
father like a shrine; other photographs of
his father in uniform, in cricket gear. The
'shrine' fades.*

33. Interior. Farmhouse: kitchen. Day.

Hugo's face.

HUGO. My dead, great, soldier-father marked me. Like bloody Hamlet. I went to Winchester Public School. I went to Cambridge University.

34. Photograph.

A Cambridge idyll, punts on the river, the camera moving away.

HUGO (*voice over*). Where I was recruited to the Intelligence Services.

35. Interior. Farmhouse. Day.

Hugo and Eddie stare at each other.

EDDIE (*shocked*). What, M.I.5 and that – ?

HUGO. That.

A silence.

EDDIE. You are telling me, that all the crap that's happened to me, the people behind it are M.I.5?

HUGO. Yes.

A silence.

EDDIE. But I'm loyal! I love my country, I love the Royal Family –

HUGO. Sadly it would appear they do not love you.

He pauses.

Now. Let me tell you of a little touch of human evil.

36. Interior. A windowless room.

The camera roams around the room. A number of men, in shirt-sleeves, coffee being drunk, before a screen, a projector. The men talk, move about, discuss. Among the men, Hugo. On the screen there is a montage of a horrifically mutilated young woman's body. She lies on crumpled sheets. Her head is severed. Shots of the head are included. Some of the pictures are in colour, others in black and white. They follow each other very quickly, dozens of them. The body is never shown in its entirety. As the camera moves about the discussion we catch glimpses on the screen of a finger, a cut piece of skin, an eye, hair over the sheets splattered in blood. The effect of this montage is of an insane, amateur butchering, slashing and cutting. The obscenity of it is shown in flashes of tiny details, never the full corpse. Near the end of the scene, look at the face of one of the men. He is weeping uncontrollably.

Music, the first movement of Bartok's 'Music for Strings, Percussion and Celeste'.

EDDIE (*voice over*). And he told me. His little touch o' human evil.

HUGO (*voice over*). She was twenty years old. The pathologists reported that everything a man could conceive of doing to a helpless woman had been done to her. Her corpse was a definitive map of every conceivable male desire.

EDDIE (*talking in the kitchen; voice over*). But who did it? Who did – did it?

HUGO (*voice over*). We never asked that.

EDDIE (*voice over*). But – But –

HUGO (*voice over*). Oh no. We never say 'but' to ourselves.

EDDIE (*voice over*). Don't get it –

HUGO (*voice over; angrily*). We are at war. You have been caught up in a nasty little operation in that war. That's all.

EDDIE (*voice over*). War, what war? War 'gainst who? Me? Chinless wonders sitting in a room runnin' a war 'gainst me? Why? Why? Haven't you got something better t' do?

HUGO (*voice over*). God how thick are you? The man who did that – atrocity. We were there to protect him. Not even to ask who he is. To find some snivelling little shit, down in the lower depths, and pin it on him. 'Set him up'. And we found you.

EDDIE (*voice over; haltingly, shocked*). The Government? The Government gave me an 'at box? What with – an 'ead in it?

A giggle.

But – I've always been a good boy.
The odd – thing on the side. But – I
mean I always vote Tory!

HUGO (*voice over*). Yes. Well. What is
happening to you is one more hard-luck
story.

EDDIE (*voice over*). You bastards –

HUGO (*voice over*). This was one more
obscene job. We were ordered not to
ask who murdered that young woman.
He is to be protected at any cost.

EDDIE (*voice over*). Yeah? Cost o'
me eh?

HUGO (*voice over*). The cost of you.

EDDIE (*voice over*). But this is England,
England!

HUGO (*voice over*). Every country needs
a few wild men, who will do anything,
anything at all, to keep the status quo.
I'm one of England's.

He pauses.

That is my vow. I will do anything for
England.

*And on the screen the last image – the
man weeping and Hugo's face,
expressionless.*

37. Interior. Farmhouse: kitchen. Day.

*Hugo and Eddie staring at each other
across the length of the table. A silence.
Then Hugo pulls at his shirt. Eddie
flinches – Hugo glares at him. Smirks.
Then takes out two photographs, large,
crumpled, from next to his body.
He throws the first down the table to
before Eddie.*

HUGO (*a sarcastic edge in his voice*).
The victim.

*Eddie picks up the photograph and
stares at it.*

Name – Mary Campbell.

Look at the large, crumpled photograph.

Aged twenty. Born in Glasgow. Came
to London when a runaway. Lived in
South London.

EDDIE. Pretty – (*He hesitates.*) – little
thing.

*Hugo throws the second photograph
to Eddie, who again stares at it. He
looks up.*

HUGO. Dana. Your ex-wife.

He smirks. Look at Eddie.

38. Insert from Episode 1, Scene 54. Interior. Dana's flat: bedroom. Night

*A brief clip of Eddie and Dana
making love.*

39. Interior. Farmhouse: kitchen. Day.

*Back to Eddie's face as he stares at the
photograph of Dana.*

HUGO. A close friend of the murdered
woman. Almost certainly involved with
the murderer. Seems our unknown
murderer, the name whom no one dares
to speak, has been knocking your wife
off. You are nearer to the greatly high
and mighty than you know, old man.

*A silence. Then Eddie goes berserk. He
overthrows the kitchen-table. He falls
over in his fury. He flies at a welsh
dresser and smashes every piece of
crockery displayed on it. A sight of
Hugo sitting calmly on his chair,
sipping whisky.*

EDDIE. Bastards! Bastards!

He runs from the kitchen.

40. Interior. Farmhouse: drawing-room. Day.

*Eddie, his bathrobe dishevelled, is
smashing the room up, his breath rasping.
He has been very thorough, it is already
badly wrecked when we join him.
Curtains torn, chairs overturned. He picks
up a poker from the fireplace. He slams
into a glass cabinet which is full of cups
and trophies. Hugo saunters into the
room and watches him for a while. Then
he draws an automatic pistol.*

HUGO. Stand where you are!

Eddie freezes.

Put your hands on the mantelpiece!

Eddie, dead still.

Do it! Now now!

Like a sleep-walker, Eddie puts his hands on the mantelpiece. Hugo goes up behind him and expertly kicks his feet apart. Then he speaks in a half-whisper, fast, into Eddie's ear.

Listen. I hate it. I have defected. I have turned on all I believe in. I cannot stand it. I tried to cry but I could not. My brain is boiling. My stomach, I have been sick, sick, sick. Understand? You lump of shit, you fall-guy, you bit of nothing out of grotty, pissy Peckham. Listen, I love my country. They are not going to do this. Not to anyone. Not to a little Scots whore off the train from Glasgow, even. Not to a petty, worthless little bit of humanity like you, even. And not to me. Not to me.

41. Interior. Farmhouse: drawing-room. Day.

Same location. A few minutes later.
Eddie still spreadeagled against the mantelpiece. Hugo, the pistol in one hand, the poker in the other, is smashing up ornaments. See from before Eddie's face, his eyes flickering nervously one way then the other as Hugo careers about the room behind him.

EDDIE (*voice over*). Dear oh dear. 'I am,' I thought, 'I am in the hands of someone right off the handle. Right off.'

Eddie tries to turn.

(*Aloud:*) Look why don't I make a cup o' tea and we'll eh, sit down an' talk this over –

But Hugo whirls on him with the gun. He holds it in both hands. His training shows. There is a knock at the door. It is Mrs Epworth, the housekeeper.

MRS EPWORTH (*off*). Mr Julian? Is that you?

Eddie and Hugo, dead still. Then Hugo relaxes.

HUGO. Yes, Mrs Epworth. Do come in.

Mrs Epworth opens the door, sees the room and stops. This as Hugo puts the gun back in his trouser belt with his back to her. He turns and smiles.

MRS EPWORTH. Oh dear.

HUGO (*charmingly*). Yes, it is a bit of a mess I'm afraid.

MRS EPWORTH. Mr Hugo. Er – the kitchen too – ?

HUGO. Yes. Mr Julian and I got back last night, with some guests. Rather a rough lot, I'm afraid.

MRS EPWORTH. Japanese gentlemen was it? Again?

HUGO. 'Fraid so.

MRS EPWORTH. And Mr Julian –

HUGO. Took them to Birmingham Airport early this morning.

MRS EPWORTH. I think I'd better call the police. We've had this kind of thing in the bedrooms before but never downstairs –

HUGO. No Mr Julian doesn't want the police called. It would not be – diplomatic, you understand?

MRS EPWORTH. Oh. No. Of course not –

HUGO. And Mr Julian will have his firm of decorators in to put things to rights.

MRS EPWORTH. Ah.

HUGO. So we'll leave things as they are.

Mrs Epworth is staring at Eddie.

It's all right. This is my driver.

MRS EPWORTH. Ah.

HUGO. So I should have the day off, Mrs Epworth.

MRS EPWORTH. Oh thank you, sir! There are things to get on with at home –

HUGO. Lovely.

MRS EPWORTH. Right. Good morning then, sir.

She slips out of the door. Eddie about to speak. Hugo puts a finger to his lips. Then opens the door. Mrs Epworth is standing there, obviously waiting to listen.

HUGO. Thank you, Mrs Epworth.

MRS EPWORTH. Thank *you*, sir.

She goes. Hugo closes the door.

HUGO. Damn. Forgot the cow comes in

on Tuesday mornings. She'll blab all over the village. Right. Clothes. Anything we need. Wait!

They stand still for a few seconds.

Go!

42. Exterior. Woodland road. Day.

Hugo walking along purposefully. A few yards behind him Eddie staggers, suitcases in either hand, weary and pissed off. Hugo turns and spins. He dances. He waves the gun about. Eddie stops still.

EDDIE (*voice over*). So off I set. On this mini-rampage. With this maniac.

(*Aloud:*) Oy.

Hugo continues to wave the gun.

Oy you!

Eddie dumps the cases down. Hugo puts the gun away and turns calmly to him.

HUGO. What, old son?

EDDIE. Why can't you carry the bloody cases? I mean, we both knocked 'em off –

Hugo runs to Eddie, who takes a step back. But Hugo, softly:

HUGO. Hush.

He points to the roadside. Tyre tracks.

Softly softly.

Reluctantly, Eddie picks up the suitcases. They follow the tyre tracks into the woods. They see a car. Hugo gestures 'Get down'. A woman's laughter. A man says something. Two lovers on the ground in the undergrowth. Hugo tries the car door. Then whips off his coat jacket. A man's voice in the undergrowth.

MAN'S VOICE. I love you, I love you, I love you!

Hugo smashes the side-window of the car. Opens the door. Gestures to Eddie to get in. Opens the bonnet. Out comes his wire with the clips. The engine starts. Eddie pushing the cases in the back of the car.

MAN'S VOICE. Love! Love! Love!

The car moves. A naked man stands up from the undergrowth.

MAN. My bloody car! My bloody car!

43. Exterior. Woodland road. Day.

The car swerving down the road. Hugo's hand waving the pistol out of the window.

EDDIE (*voice over*). Madness. Madness. Sunny days.

44. Exterior. Small village. Day.

Eddie and Hugo leaving the car. Eddie nervous, looking around with the suitcases. They set off down the sleepy main street.

They come to a small sweetshop-cum-grocers. Hugo stops. Eddie bumps into him. Hugo nods at the shop. They go in.

45. Interior. Village shop. Day.

A very small little girl in a dirty blue frock stands, thumb in mouth, a doll hanging from the other hand, staring at them. There is no one else in the shop. Hugo goes to the till, leans over, rings it open, takes out all the money, pockets it, closes the till. The little girl stares.

Just as Hugo closes the till an old man shuffles into the shop. A kindly face.

OLD MAN. Can I help you, m'ducks?

HUGO (*royally*). Yes. Could I please have a tin of red salmon?

OLD MAN. Oh, ooh, I – ar.

He finds a tin on the shelf. Eddie, meanwhile, staring the little girl in the eye. She does not take the thumb out of her mouth.

Ar. That'll be one pound fifty p.

He hands the tin to Hugo, who hands him two one-pound notes. The old man rings up the till. He stares into it.

OLD MAN. 'Fraid I be out a' change. Awful sorry.

HUGO. No trouble. Give her some sweets.

The stare of the little girl. Eddie, sweating with fear.

46. Exterior. Marshy pond in the middle of a copse. Day.

Hugo and Eddie pushing the car down a slope. It runs ahead of them, into the pond. It sticks, pathetically. Hugo raves.

HUGO. Bloody England! Bloody bloody England! No bloody lake to bury a car! No bloody patch of earth to bury a corpse where it won't be found! Bloody bloody England!

He crouches, holding his face in his hands.

EDDIE. Look. Look –

Hugo snaps out of it. Stands.

HUGO. Lunchtime.

EDDIE. What?

HUGO. We're not going to open the bloody salmon are we. No tin opener. Classic predicament of the picnic! Don't worry I know a pub near here.

47. Exterior. Country scene near a pub. Day.

A blast of music. Carrying suitcases, Hugo and Eddie are running, crouched toward a hedge. They kneel, opening the suitcases, pulling out clothes.
The camera leaves them and goes over the hedge. The music stops. Birdsong, the clink of glasses, laughter and talk. It is a swish country pub, drinkers out on tables on the grass in the sunshine, expensive cars parked. Move amongst the drinkers.

1ST MALE DRINKER. Four hundred thousand.

2ND MALE DRINKER. Absolutely.

Move to another group.

1ST WOMAN DRINKER. A sweet thing. A darling. I love her.

2ND WOMAN DRINKER. Are you talking about your horse or your daughter?

Laughter. Move to another group.

3RD MALE DRINKER. I mean, there's hardly any cover there. For the birds. Then all these bloody lawyers come out from Birmingham and bang away, unable even to kill the bloody pheasants. I mean it's a farce.

4TH MALE DRINKER. Then there's the problem with inexperienced beaters –

3RD MALE DRINKER. Sloshed out of their minds –

5TH MALE DRINKER. More fun to shoot the beaters –

Laughs.

3RD MALE DRINKER. I don't think it's funny anymore, there isn't any decent shooting a hundred miles this side of Birmingham –

Move to another group.

SANDRA. Swopped a Toyota for a little MG – mind you the Japs make those too now don't they?

CLIVE. Don't know, still British – just, I think. I had an MG when I was up at Jesus –

Hugo and Eddie walk amongst these drinkers. Hugo is in smart slacks and a pale-blue pullover with an open-necked shirt. Eddie is wearing an ill-fitting sports jacket and a cloth cap. Eddie is nervous, Hugo confident and at ease.

CLIVE. My God, Hugo. Hugo! What are you doing here?

HUGO. Heard the beer was good. How are you Clive?

CLIVE. Surviving the massacre. Uncanny. I was just mentioning the old place. (*To the woman:*) Hugo and I were up at Jesus together. Hugo, Sandra.

SANDRA. Hello.

HUGO. Hello.

Clive, a nod at Eddie.

Oh, this is my man.

CLIVE. Oh.

Clive ignores Eddie from now on.

CLIVE. I must warn you, Sandra, Hugo is an utter shit.

SANDRA. Interesting.

48. Exterior. Pub. Day.

Same location.
As they drink, Eddie looks at the drinkers outside the pub. He studies their

lips, the wobbles of cheeks, hair-cuts, the edges of women's skirts, the marks of wealth. He is mesmerised. Snatches of the conversation between Hugo and his friends.

EDDIE (*voice over*). The silver spoon in the tonsils. I felt small. I worried I was smelly. It began t'get to me.

CLIVE (*to Sandra*). Do you know what this man did at Cambridge? Lead us all on a house-breaking expedition. Never been more terrified in my life.

SANDRA. How much did you steal?

HUGO. Enough.

SANDRA. Enough for what?

HUGO. To feel alive.

SANDRA. I see.

She eyes him, slyly.

EDDIE (*voice over*). This lot. Looked like different animals to me. Martians? Been beamed down, taken the bloody country over, with none of us noticin'? Out o' my depth? That don' say it all. Naked, I felt. Naked. And the beer was that real ale muck.

Eddie draining a pint in one go, then grimacing, as he looks at the details of faces and dress. He finishes, smacks his lips, grimaces.

HUGO (*to Eddie*). Don't get pissed. Will you, 'Burt'.

EDDIE. What? Oh. No. 'Sir'.

SANDRA (*eyeing Eddie*). 'Burt'. What is that short for?

EDDIE. Nebuchadnezzar.

They stare at Eddie.

CLIVE. Got a servant problem, Hugo?

HUGO. Nothing I can't handle.

Hugo drawing Clive aside.

Can I have a word old man?

They walk away. Sandra looks daggers at them for leaving her. She turns to 'Burt'.

SANDRA. Well. 'Burt'. And what interests you in life?

EDDIE (*shrugs*). Giving your bum a bite?

SANDRA. What a sexist, working-class little turd you are, 'Burt'.

EDDIE. Sorry. Don't understand the insult, darling.

SANDRA. You feel insulted?

EDDIE. Funny how you lot keep on talking about how you 'feel'.

SANDRA (*shrugs, in imitation of Eddie*). But we are the idle rich. What else is there to do but 'feel'?

EDDIE. You've lost me, darlin'.

SANDRA. Oh. Pity. I thought I was going to feel your teeth in my bum. Bye-bye.

She wanders away to Clive, and leans against him. Eddie watches her go.

EDDIE (*low*). Oh my God.

(*Voice over.*) After that I got a bit lost.

Dissolve into:

49. Exterior. Pub. Day.

Near closing time. Seen from a drunken Eddie's point of view. He is lying on the grass outside the pub looking up at the sky. Hugo, Clive and Sandra come up to him. He pours a pint of beer clumsily over his lips. It runs down his neck.

EDDIE. Sorry –

CLIVE (*echoey, to Eddie's hearing*). Real ale old boy, can't take it.

SANDRA. Silly little man –

CLIVE. You find him horribly attractive you shameless bitch –

SANDRA. Do I?

HUGO (*close to Eddie*). 'Burt'. 'Burt'. We're going to Clive's place.

EDDIE. Er?

50. Exterior. Road. Day.

From Eddie's point of view. They are carrying Eddie to the back of an estate wagon and put him in it. He wriggles.

EDDIE. I! I! Am the mosht wanted – man n'in the country!

CLIVE. Yes yes yes, God Hugo you do pick 'em –

51. Interior. The back of the estate wagon. Day.

From Eddie's point of view. He is laid out, with difficulty, in the back of the estate.

EDDIE (*into Clive's face*). Thish – thish – the planet Mars?

CLIVE. Herefordshire, old son. Herefordshire.

He slams the back of the estate and Eddie passes out – so the screen dissolves to black.

52. Interior. Small room over stables. Late evening.

Eddie wakes up with a start, so the image of a small, round window, divided by a cross, is suddenly there. The room has low eaves, a washstand, a single, iron-frame bed. No other furniture. A picture hanging on the wall, a dim old print. A single bulb, unshaded, hanging over the bed.
Eddie shifts. Looks about him. He moves. He realises his right ankle is handcuffed to the bottom of the bed. He looks down. He has no trousers on.

EDDIE. Oh no.

A pause.

No! No! No!

He thrashes about on the bed. He hits his head on the iron head of the bed. He passes out, so the screen dissolves to black.

53. Interior. Small room over stables. Night.

Later.
A full moon at the little round window.
Eddie wakes. He sees the moon, it shines along his body on the bed. He moves his head from side to side, looking at the window. It divides the moon, like a target. He twists on the bed slowly, in discomfort. He leans over, feeling beneath the bed. He watches his hand lift an old-fashioned chamber pot, a blue scene around its side – he stares at it. Dimly in the moonlight, shepherds and shepherdesses are seen, with sheep beneath trees.
Look at his face as he urinates in the chamber pot. He closes his eyes in misery.

EDDIE (*voice over*). I thought to myself – I deserve this. I do.

(*Aloud:*) I'm sorry I've lived a bad life, God.

(*Voice over:*) Y'know. The things you think when you're pissed.

(*Aloud:*) Oh. Oh.

He puts the chamber pot back under the bed – not shown, the sound, on bare floorboards. Stay looking at Eddie's face. Moonlight. He looks at the window. Show it.

Bloody moonlight.

He passes out. The window, the moon at its centre, dissolves to black.

54. Interior. Small room over stables. Night.

Eddie wakes. Sees first the window, the moon gone. Stars. Then a strange light in the room. He looks toward the door – do not show his face, just what he sees. Sandra stands in the doorway. She wears a white, Victorian nightdress. The light is from a 'gaz' lamp – harsh, white, shadows swinging as it dangles from her hand.
She looks at him. She moves into the room, leans against the wall. She pulls the door closed. She strikes a pose. Puts out her tongue. Then she is rubbing one foot against the other, awkwardly.

SANDRA. You're not going to believe this. I had to come through the yard so I've got my wellingtons on. And I can't get the bloody things off.

Look at Eddie's face for the first time in the scene.

EDDIE. Oh dear.

His eyes look her up and down.

My love.

55. Interior. Small room over stables. Night.

Later.
Eddie and Sandra have made love. They lie naked on the bed. The lamp is on the floor. Deep shadows. Eddie is still handcuffed by his right ankle. Sandra is smoking, giving Eddie a puff. They shift awkwardly on the narrow bed.

SANDRA. They're talking about you, over there.

EDDIE. Yeah? Over where?

SANDRA. In the house.

EDDIE. What house?

SANDRA. Ludlow Hall. Don't you know where you are?

EDDIE. Not really.

He sighs. Reaches for the cigarette.

SANDRA. You're in one of the rooms over the stables, of Ludlow Hall.

EDDIE. Oh.

SANDRA. I mean – do you know who Clive is?

EDDIE. ?

SANDRA. Hugo's – I mean, your friend's friend. He's Lord Ludlow.

EDDIE. Oh.

A pause.

What do you want me to do? Faint?

SANDRA. Clive, the Lord Ludlow. Who embezzled one million pounds from ICI. Who was never prosecuted, because of the scandal. I mean he's forty-ninth in succession to the bloody throne of England.

EDDIE. Oh dear.

A pause.

So Her Majesty –

SANDRA. He'll never do a day's work again, darling. Not even for the RSPCA. That's his punishment.

EDDIE. Unemployment?

SANDRA. Sad isn't it. And he's so young.

EDDIE. Yeah. (*Lost.*) Very sad. Very.

SANDRA. So, Eddie.

She kisses him.

EDDIE (*moving his head back from her*). Er, I thought my name was 'Burt'.

SANDRA. I've been listening at the door. Hugo and Clive talking.

EDDIE. Oh.

SANDRA. They think you know who killed her.

EDDIE (*frozen*). ?

SANDRA. They think you know – the name – of the man who killed – Mary Campbell. Be – careful, my love. I mean tell them.

EDDIE. Tell 'em what?

SANDRA. All I'm saying is that when Clive asks you a question, whatever you do, say yes.

EDDIE (*pauses, then gutteral*). How d'you mean –

SANDRA (*she puts her finger to his lips*). If Clive the Lord Ludlow applied to join the SAS, he wouldn't get in. On grounds of unacceptable violence.

EDDIE. Oh –

And she puts her finger into his mouth. He nearly chokes. She suddenly pulls her finger from his mouth, whirling round and sitting up on the side of the bed.

SANDRA. Sorry. That million Clive embezzled. (*A little laugh.*) He is not, exactly, ever going to pay it back! And he and I are going to get married. So.

EDDIE (*turning to embrace her from behind*). Look love, I don't know what – (*But his handcuffed right foot prevents him.*) Oh God this thing – eh! It's beginning t' bleed!

SANDRA. What do you want me to be? The naked girl in your life with the key?

(*She pauses.*) Thank you.

EDDIE (*embarrassed*). Well. Thank you, love –

SANDRA (*standing*). The lamp's running out of gas, I'm going. If I don't I'll fall over in the shit in the yard –

EDDIE. Yeah –

She picks up the lamp and her nightdress and wellingtons and goes, quickly, slamming the door. The room suddenly dark. Eddie looks at the star-defined outline of the round window. He falls asleep. The screen dissolves to black.

(*Voice over:*) Long night of the knives, eh? The pleasure, then the pain?

56. Interior. Small room over stables. Night.

The starlit round window, for a second. Then the bulb above the small bed is switched on – a click. Hugo and Clive are in the room, looking down on the naked Eddie. They each carry an opened bottle of champagne. Clive is smoking a cigar. He stumbles. A crash.

CLIVE. I've kicked the bloody ice bucket over!

HUGO (*closing his eyes*). Please, Clive, are we going to do this or not?

Clive falls on his knees, from Eddie's view, doing something on the floor – he's picking up ice cubes.

Clive has this idea, Eddie, of torture. Ice on the skin, then a burning cigar. He claims he learnt this from a mercenary who fought in Rhodesia. I must say it all sounds highly exotic to me.

EDDIE (*raising himself on his elbows*). Wha? Wha?

HUGO. Myself, I think he got it from an old James Bond movie. Which I think I dimly remember.

Clive appears at the bottom of the bed with a grunt, dumping a champagne bucket on the sheet beside Eddie's feet. With his left foot, Eddie sends it flying.

CLIVE. Oh you shit!

He falls backwards out of view.

EDDIE (*raising himself up, writhing on the bed*). Wotcha, wotcha, wotcha – gonna do?

Dissolve quickly to –

57. Interior. Small room above stables. Night.

Close to Eddie's face, sweat bursting in beads from his skin, screaming. Dissolve into black.

58. Interior. Small room over stables. Dawn.

Dissolve up into the round window flooded by sunlight. Close to Eddie's face. He blinks at the brilliant window. He squints. He sees Hugo. He flinches with fear. Hugo looks at him. He is exhausted. He raises the champagne bottle to his lips. The bottle is long empty. He holds it out upside down. His arm flops.

HUGO (*never looking at Eddie in this scene*). Anything for England.

EDDIE (*raising his head*). My leg –

HUGO. Clive's gone. I think you may have destroyed him. You do know the man who killed Mary Campbell, Eddie. The man I – set out to protect. You do.

EDDIE (*tears*). I – I – I –

HUGO. No please, please don't – I'm not going to start on you again. Please. But –

He pauses, looking out of the small window.

Somewhere in you, you know. You've seen who he is. I must know. I must.

Low, an insane note in his voice.

For bloody England –

EDDIE. I –

HUGO (*turning, pulling at his trouser pocket and then producing the handcuff key*). Look I – here.

He undoes the handcuff. Then turns away. Eddie sits up.

EDDIE. Oh. Oh. Lovely. Ta.

HUGO. We're renegades, Eddie.

EDDIE. My leg.

HUGO. You know who killed her, Eddie. Deep down. You must. He's had your wife! He could do what he did to that young woman, to Dana –

EDDIE. Look at my leg.

Show Eddie's right leg for the first time. It is covered in burns. Hugo looks down at it.

HUGO. Forgive me, I –

EDDIE. I thought you knew who he was. That was why I hung around –

A gesture.

Then you set that madman on me –

HUGO. Clive's – not around now. I – we've got the run of the place. Here – I'll help you over to the house.

He pauses.

Forgive.

He still has not looked Eddie in the eyes.

59. Voice over these scenes.

EDDIE (*voice over*). So I lay about. Must have been, oh a week. Like a Lord. Just staring at the countryside. Mildly pissed. Mildly this an' that. Didn't see much of Hugo. He was there. Sort of ashamed. Dunno what he was up to. Waitin' for 'em to come and get us. Out o' the picture postcard, outside o' the window.

Over:

60. Exterior. Country house: forecourt. Day.

A huge eighteenth-century country house: steps, classical pillars; massive windows (e.g. Berrington Hall). A limping Eddie is being helped toward the house. Look at it, with a blast of music from the front. A butler stands waiting in attendance on the steps.

61. Exterior. Country house: gardens. Day.

Eddie sitting, wrapped up, by a wrought-iron, white table, in the grounds, the house behind him. The butler is approaching with drinks.

62. Exterior. Window of the country house. Day.

Eddie sitting in a window, looking out. Move towards him.

63. Interior. The windowseat. Day.

Eddie sitting, in an elaborate dressing-gown, looking out of the window. Travel to him across a grandly furnished room.

Dissolve to:

64. Interior. The window seat/exterior. Grounds. Day.

Eddie dressed, sipping a Scotch. Hugo comes into the room, dressed in hunting clothes.

EDDIE. What's goin' on?

HUGO. Ludlow and County Hunt. Bit of a risk, but I thought I'd go out. How are you?

EDDIE. Your schoolboy torture's beginnin' to itch.

He is looking out of the window. Men and women on horseback are milling about. Red and black coats. The butler moves amongst them, serving toddies. He looks at one particular woman. He looks again. It's Dana. She is beautifully dressed in hunting gear, utterly confident on the horse.

65. Flashback insert.

A kaleidoscope of images of Dana, starting with the crumpled photograph, then of close-ups of her from the first episode.

66. Interior. The window seat. Day.

EDDIE. Jesus bloody Christ.

HUGO. What's the matter?

Eddie pulls his head, by the neck to the window.

EDDIE. Dana.

HUGO. Who's she with?

EDDIE. My Dana.

HUGO. Eddie!

EDDIE. Looking like a million dollars, the bitch –

HUGO. Eddie! She could be with him. Guests come and ride at the hunt. Girlfriends, the odd high-class whore. I knew it. This is my world. I knew he'd bring her here. Heart of England –

He rushes to the door.

The bastard has brought his whore to the hunt. I'll track her. You just stay here.

He goes.

67. Exterior. Steps of the country house. Day.

Eddie hobbles out onto the steps. The hunt is riding off over the fields.
The blast of music.

EDDIE (*shouts*). Dana!

He runs down the steps.

68. Exterior. Fields. Day.

A sequence.
Eddie, on foot, scrambling through hedges. The hunt is always two or three fields away, or glimpsed the other side of woodland. The sound of horses' hoofs, the hunting horn's call. Close to us, the sound of Eddie's breathless panting, sometimes an exhausted moan as he blunders about the countryside.

EDDIE (*voice over*). Now I saw 'em, now I didn't. They seemed to go round and round. Stuck her on a horse, had he? In shiny boots, had he, the bastard. He must be loaded. Course he's loaded, I thought! They're all loaded! Loaded with it!

69. Exterior. A field with a high hedgerow. Day.

He stumbles and falls on the grass. He looks up. Dana rides slowly toward him. She looks down. He squints up, sun in his eyes.

DANA. Just over the hedge, Eddie.

She spurs the horse; it gallops and they jump through the hedge.

70. Exterior. Small field. Day.

It is triangular in shape, the hedgerows are high, making it secluded. Dana waits on her horse.

DANA. Here.

She takes a small leather bag hanging from her saddle and throws it to him.

EDDIE. What's this?

DANA. Lot of money, Eddie.

EDDIE. Bloody whore!

DANA. Stay away from me, Eddie. Don't think about me. Don't look for me. They know what you're doing all the time. You can never win, Eddie, love.

EDDIE. He killed someone, Dana! Mary Campbell. You knew her for Christ's sake Dana – who is he?

DANA. Stay away from me.

She looks about the field, anxiously.

EDDIE. Who – ?

He whirls around – follow his gaze, zigzagging along the hedgerows. Suddenly Hugo's horse jumps through the hedge. He dismounts and runs toward Eddie shouting.

HUGO. Grab her bridle! Eddie, grab the bridle!

Dana spurs her horse and gallops away down the field. Eddie shouts at Hugo.

EDDIE. Hugo no!

And two men in black, with black balaclavas come out of the hedge with automatic weapons. They shoot Hugo dead.
And are standing in front of Eddie. The three of them, dead still. Then one of the masked men picks up the leather bag and casually tosses it to Eddie. He catches the bag. He backs away. The gunmen stand still. He turns and runs.

71. Exterior. Country road. Evening.

*Blast of music. Eddie is running, in a bad
state, his limp making him slip toward
the ditch on the side of the road. He
pauses for breath. Go close to him. He
hears motorbikes coming. He scrambles
into the ditch.*
  *Two police motorbikes pass him. They
are escorting a huge black limousine. As
it passes, through the side window, he
catches a glimpse of – Dana.*

  *End of Episode 2.
  Blank screen.*

*Over the credits a heavy-metal
rendering of:*

  Pussycat pussycat
  Where have you been?
  I've been to London
  to see the Queen.

  Pussycat pussycat
  What did you there?
  I frightened a mouse
  Under her chair.

Episode 3

The War-Room

Episode 3

Characters

EDDIE CASS	Denis Lawson
CARACTACUS	Norman Beaton
JILL	Susannah Bunyan
STOKER	Larrington Walker
SLEEPER	Winston Crooke
OLD WOMAN	Helen McCarthy
WESLEY	Alan Cooke

i EDDIE sees JILL in a Birmingham pub.
EDDIE: 'My paranoia went right up and hit the bell.'

ii EDDIE drying-out in Bristol.

iii EDDIE: 'Hello Stoker. Got a parcel for me?'

1. Blank screen.

EDDIE (*voice over*). What is life? Or put that another way. What is money?

2. Interior. Derelict room. Night.

A bottle fills the screen. Light splinters through it.

EDDIE (*voice over*). Power, money is power. Turn it to whisky-power over your brain.

Eddie's face – red-veined eye-balls flickering.

3. Reprise.

Stills and very brief clips of the first and second episodes.

EDDIE (*voice over*). Without power, no bloody life at all, eh?

So money is life.

Yeah. I was kind o' proud o' that thought. The condition I was in.

Life power money, money power life. Seemed the whole key to what was being done to me.

What really got me was – that wherever I was – whatever hole in the ground, there was someone up there, wanted me there.

Like a slippery pole.

He was up there, sitting on the top. I'd get a few feet up to him – and slither! Back down I went. And I think I saw 'im and all.

Ending the sequence with the black car, Dana in the back, that Eddie glimpses on the road.

Well, his car. My ex-wife in the back.

I could not stop seeing that car.

The image of the car, distorting.

It was 'the man'.

4. Interior. Small derelict room. Night.

The whisky bottle again, then Eddie's face, then the room. It is lit by a camping gaz. Camping equipment lies around the room. Amongst it a small barbeque set.

EDDIE (*voice over*). Made it to Birmingham.

Went into a Millets – campin' equipment, I thought. Since I was goin' to be on my own. Got myself a little barbeque, even. (*He fiddles with it, lost.*)

Since I had ten grand, didn't see why I shouldn't go on the run in luxury.

A rat runs across the floor. Eddie recoils in horror. Then looks suspiciously at the whisky bottle, suspecting DTs.

Birmingham. Rat city. Three days walkin' to make it there. Derelict house.

A flash of the rat again. Eddie throws the bottle: a loud crash and scamperings.
    Close to it, on the dirty floorboards, a piece of glass wobbles, wet with the whisky.
    In the distance, a police siren begins.
    He scrambles to the gaz lamp and turns it down, his eyes looking at the window in terror.

5. Interior. Betting shop. Day.

Close-up of pages of Sporting Life.

EDDIE (*voice over*). Money is power. Power is life. Therefore money is life.

Yeah! If only I could get the right philosophy, I thought, in the end I'll screw 'em.

6. Interior. Betting shop. Day.

Eddie, money being paid out to him. He wears dark glasses. On his back, his camping gear. Close – the hard eye of the man paying out, the impenetrable black of Eddie's glasses.

EDDIE (*voice over*). So I went investin'.

7. Interior. Betting shop. Day.

The Sun *newspaper. The front-page must be about Margaret Thatcher. Eddie turns the page, briefly lingers on the 'page three' model, then turns to the racing page. Close to the print, going down the day's runners.*

EDDIE (*voice over*). And, to my amazement, got in step with the universe. My philosophy worked! Money attracts money. Life attracts life.

8. Interior. Betting shop. Day.

Eddie, dressed as before, dark glasses, being paid out more money. The steely eye of the man paying out unreadable. Eddie smiles at him.

9. Interior. Derelict room. Night.

Eddie, going again, to a distant police siren, to turn down the gaz lamp.

EDDIE (*voice over*). But always the thought – they are letting me do this. They are riggin' the horses, to get me rich. I am bein' fattened up again. They – want – me – here –

The look of terror again, as he glances at the window.

I knew I only had to wait, an' the world'd be in touch with me again.

10. Interior. Public bar. Birmingham. Night.

A small, poor, bar-room. All but Eddie are black. Eddie, dark glasses on, sits in the corner at a small table, pint of beer before him. His camping gear is by his side.

EDDIE (*voice over*). It was the Queen Mother's birthday. I had to drink her health.

He raises his glass. He drinks and stops. Into the bar comes Jill on the arm of a West Indian man. They sit down. The man goes to the bar to get drinks. Eddie drinks on. He looks at her.

Jill.

11. Flashback to Episode 1, Scene 26. Night. Interior Caractacus's room.

From Episode 1: Jill shouting at Eddie from her bed on the floor in Caractacus's room. Very briefly.

12. Interior. Birmingham pub. Night.

Eddie observing Jill, who has not noticed him. She is looking down, opening a handbag, taking out cigarettes, a lighter. Then she is lighting a cigarette.

EDDIE (*voice over*). My old friend Caractacus's bit. In Birmingham. My paranoia went right up and hit the bell.

13. Flashback to Episode 1, Scene 26. Night. Interior. Caractacus's room.

Again, very briefly, Jill in Caractacus's room, rising from the bed.
   A blast of the brass music.

14. Interior. Birmingham pub. Night.

The man brings drinks to Jill's table. Eddie takes off his glasses. Jill drinks – then sees Eddie.
   Their stares cross and recross the bar-room.
   Jill turns to the man and argues standing to leave. He protests, holds her arm. She pulls it away. He shrugs – she walks out of the bar, quickly. This is seen through Eddie's eyes – and, partly, through his dark glasses.
   Eddie lifts his pack and walks out of the bar.

15. Exterior. Pavements, walls, corners. Night.

Jill is seen briefly turning corners – looking back, going another way. Her shadow on tin hoarding. Eddie chases her. This is a montage – flickering, brief glimpses. Eddie panting, stopping, listening. Traffic – then another glimpse.

EDDIE (*voice over*). Is every city in the bloody country the same at night? Bashed up streets, dirty walls?

Every city in the world? New York, Moscow, Beirut, Birmingham – yeah, in a back street somewhere – a man runnin' after a woman.

For some reason or other.

Everywhere's a' same. Everywhere, same as bloody nowhere.

16. Exterior. Birmingham back street. Night.

Eddie catches Jill against some railings. Beyond, deep dark of a patch of wasteground and the city lights. He pushes her against the railings, holding her.

JILL. Bugger off!

EDDIE. Where is he? Caractacus? Tell me!

A small, round-bodied old woman is suddenly standing by them. She has a panting, elderly, fat little dog on a lead.

OLD WOMAN (*Birmingham accent*). Even if you don't love her, there's no need to do that to her.

EDDIE. What?

OLD WOMAN. It's disgusting. Whatever happened to romance?

EDDIE. Yeah, thank you darlin'.

Eddie walks away, holding Jill hard by the arm. The old woman standing, glaring at them.

Where is Caractacus? Here in Brummy land?

OLD WOMAN (*shouting, from a distance*). Modern love? You can keep it!

JILL. What's it to you –

EDDIE. Do you know about me? You know what's happenin' to me? You know who I am now?

JILL. Gone up in the world, have you Eddie?

EDDIE. Oh you remember my name.

They glare at each other. Violence in Eddie's face.

JILL. He's in St Paul's.

EDDIE. Where?

JILL. Bristol.

EDDIE. Bristol. Well! (*He looks at his watch.*) The night is young. We'll get a train. New Street.

JILL. Get lost.

EDDIE. I'm not letting you out o' my sight.

JILL. I've not got my things.

EDDIE. Buy you a toothbrush on the station.

17. Exterior. New Street Station. Night.

Close to Eddie's face. Behind it, Jill – she holds a paper bag up to her face, hand dipping into it, taking out a bottle of nail varnish. Behind them, the bright façade of a station Boots chemist.
Eddie, eyes flickering.

EDDIE (*voice over*). Railway station. A public place, but a kind o' private hell for me.

EDDIE (*speaks*). What you buy all that stuff in there for?

JILL. Said you were goin' to buy me a toothbrush.

EDDIE. Eyeblushers? False nails? You set me back seventy quid!

JILL. If I'm leaving bloody Birmingham for a holiday in bloody Bristol, I want to feel good. Right?

EDDIE. Right! (*He shrugs, nonplussed.*) Right –

JILL (*going out of view*). Come on! We'll miss the train!

18. Interior. First-class railway carriage. Night.

The train in motion. Eddie and Jill sitting opposite each other. A solitary businessman sits across the aisle, papers out, briefcase open.
Eddie in a half-whisper. Jill aloud.

EDDIE. First class?

JILL. If you want to kidnap me and screw me rotten in Bristol, we are goin' first class.

*The businessman glares at her. Jill
gives him a single finger 'V' – sign.
The businessman sighs, throws the
papers in his briefcase and moves
away. Jill smiles at Eddie then wipes
the smile off her face.
Wipe to:*

19. Interior. First-class railway carriage. Night.

*Later.
Jill is making her face up. Eddie is
looking at her over a dozen cans of
Ruddles beer from the buffet, some opened.
He pulls the ring off another can.*

EDDIE. When did you see him last?
Caractacus?

JILL (*insolently*). You what?

Eddie sips.

EDDIE (*voice over*). Oh yeah, modern
love. Modern times. I fancied her
something rotten. Something about
being in danger – really makes you
want to get it on.
(*Aloud:*) Huh huh!

JILL. Oh get lost.

*Look at Eddie, sipping from the can
again.*

EDDIE (*voice over*). Yup, modern love,
modern times.
(*Aloud:*) Talk to me!

He slams his can down on the table.

That night they busted you, me and
Caractacus. What they say to you?
Why did you clear out? I went back –
it was full of muscle. Eddie's brothers.
Look! This is to do with my life!

JILL. Don't want to know about your life.

She pauses.

Don't mind goin' to Bristol, though.

20. Blank screen.

EDDIE (*voice over*). Lives. Lives. On
this tiny island. All tangled up.

A chuckle.

A real bowl o' spaghetti.

21. Exterior. Street in St Pauls, Bristol, before a café. Night.

*Eddie and Jill looking up and down the
street. Everyone in the street and in the
café, but for Eddie and Jill, is black.*

EDDIE (*voice over*). All tangled up.
Sometimes I feel – which bit o'
spaghetti am I, then?

Eddie and Jill turn to go into the café.

22. Interior. Café. Night.

*It is packed and noisy. Eddie and Jill sit
uncomfortably, sharing a chair.*

EDDIE. I'll get a cup of tea –

JILL. Stay where you are. Just wait.

*The men and women at the table burst
into laughter at a joke. A man – it is
the sleeper whom Eddie met in
Caractacus's basement flat –
approaches.*

SLEEPER. Hello Jill.

JILL. He's – (*indicating Eddie.*) with me.

SLEEPER. Mr – Eddie – Cass.

23. Flashback to Episode 1, Scene 33.

*The sleeper confronting Eddie, giving him
the letter from Caractacus.*

24. Interior. Café. Night.

EDDIE. Don't I know you?

SLEEPER. Ah. A question of philosophy,
my friend, deep, deep philosophy.

EDDIE. Or spaghetti.

SLEEPER (*face closer to Eddie*). Not
with you, friend.

JILL. Shut up Eddie. (*To the sleeper:*) Is
he around?

SLEEPER. Let us – retire for some
refreshment.

He walks away.

JILL. Come!

*Jill takes Eddie by the hand and leads
him after the sleeper to a door at the
back of the café.*

25. Interior. No windows. Back room of café.

A pool table. Low, shadowy light. Caractacus is leaning over the table, playing. A few small tables, drinkers. Bottles of rum and coke. Caractacus straightens, leans against the table, relaxed, laughs. Jill goes to him. They embrace, then turn, arms around each other, and look at Eddie.

EDDIE (*voice over*). Dear oh dear. When you meet a couple who're having it, s'horrible how, sometimes, they just look utterly evil.

CARACTACUS. How you doing, Eddie?

EDDIE. Caractacus, I – I dunno how to put this. But, but – (*Struggling with his back pack, he pauses.*)

CARACTACUS. But what, boy?

EDDIE. I am on my uppers. My feet and hands up in the air. In the crapola. Sinking, very fast.

CARACTACUS. Truly sorry to hear that, boy. Sounds like you's not eating healthy food –

EDDIE (*shouts*). Caractacus! You black bastard!

He sweeps the pool balls off the end, around the table. Show them, from low down, bouncing amongst people's feet. Then cut to – everyone standing in the room. A silence.

You ran out on me. You disappeared – into the mists. And I been drownin' ever since. Strangled in spaghetti!

Look at Caractacus – eyebrows raised at this display.

Now you – you – help me.

Eddie wilts.

CARACTACUS. Brothers, sisters, I jus' want to play some pool with this lunatic. I jus' want to play some pool.

Arms extended to Eddie. Eddie embraces him.

You all go downstairs, for a while, while I play some pool, with this lunatic.

A pause. Then it is clear that Caractacus has given an order. The drinkers relax and begin to move.

26. Interior. Back room of café. No windows.

A little later.
The room is empty, but for Jill, who sits at a table in the shadows, drinking rum and coke. The table is set for a game of pool. Eddie and Caractacus, with cues.

EDDIE. Big man round here, are you?

CARACTACUS. No one man or woman is big. We are all servants of the Lord God. (*He tosses a coin.*) Call.

EDDIE. Oh. Tails.

He loses. Caractacus laughs and begins to play, quickly, without fault.

27. Interior. Back room of café. No windows.

The pool table seen from above – a sequence of wipes as Caractacus clears the table three times, moving quickly and expertly round it.

EDDIE (*voice over*). I told him. The parcel. The head. The nightmare. The upper-class twit Hugo. The horror at a hunt, in the English countryside. The guns from nowhere, out of the English hedges. Money from nowhere. And the man in a car – with Dana.

Big black car.

Eddie blinks. For a flash he sees the black car, like a gleaming model resting in the middle of the pool table. Blinks – it is gone.

And Caractacus just played. My old freaky companion in petty crime – had changed.

He was hard, balanced. Something fit about him. There was power there.

'Is he listening at all?' I thought. 'Or is he just zonked out, playing pool?'

People do change, for the worse. Or the better.

Someone you've known for years can suddenly be a stranger.

Like Dana.

Or me.

God, what was I turning into?

The sequence ends with Caractacus

*ceremonially potting the black ball.
Look at Jill. She smokes. A slight
shake of her hand as she raises the
cigarette. Look at Eddie. There is
sweat on his face.*

EDDIE (*aloud*). That's it. Story o' my
adventures. (*He shrugs.*) Help me.

*Caractacus's face, unsmiling, looking
at him. A silence.*

CARACTACUS. Boy. (*He pauses.*) I
knew that bust, at my place, that night,
was phoney.

He pauses.

Boy, I never been so frightened in my
life. They weren't no filth. Those
bastards – they were something else.

EDDIE. But what they say to you?

CARACTACUS. Martians boy! Off the
planet. Forces of darkness –

JILL (*suddenly, out of the dark*). They
didn't take us to a cop-shop. They took
us down some waste ground.

CARACTACUS. Greatly abused us.
Greatly. Forces of darkness –

JILL. *I've* never been so frightened in my
life. Think –

*The nervousness with the cigarette, her
face shaded.*

How I felt in Brum. Walkin' into a
pub, seeing you.

CARACTACUS. What they say? To
have nothing to do with you, man.
Nothing at all. You's leprosy. You's a
nuclear-war victim, ra-di-ation, touch
you and we blind. Nothing to do with
you, ever.

*Eddie's sweating face. Jill leans into
the light.*

JILL. Ever.

EDDIE. Yeah? Makes me kind o'
irresistible, don't it, darlin'!

JILL (*leaning back into the darkness*).
Don't count on it.

EDDIE (*his face is now beaded all over
with sweat, it drips from his brow,
from his chin – lit from above, the
sweat gleaming, his face contorted*).
I told you! Who they are!
The government!

*And Caractacus's face, leaning back
from the light into the dark.*

You got a believe me! The government
is comin' for me! Personally! Little
crapiola me!

CARACTACUS (*his face in the dark*).
Boy, I've had my brushes with the
English Government. I've done time.
I've had prison screws, I've had the
DHSS walking all over me. This don't
sound like any of 'em to me.

EDDIE (*the super-sweating face again,
contorting*). Don't you understand,
s'different! They are lookin' after their
own! One o' their own! Who's done
somethin'! They're really comin' out o'
the walls!

(*Suddenly light:*) Ha! They don't have
to, usually y'see – usually s'all dandy.
Bit of a poke, kick up the arse in a cop
shop – nothin' at all. But – (*Panicking:*)
When they're really up against it, they
got guns, they got – the whole bloody
country in their pocket. They'll use –
flame-throwers if they got to!

He closes his eyes.

Please. You got to believe me. You're
the nearest thing I got – to a friend.

CARACTACUS (*in the dark*). Boy, you
don't need to tell this black brother
what they're capable of.

He leans into the light, and is smiling.

Eddie, I do see now, you's fighting a
holy war. I do believe you's fighting a
holy war.

EDDIE (*wiping his face*). Oh yeah! That
what I'm doing?

CARACTACUS. A – holy – war. Know
why you're doing badly?

EDDIE (*wiping his face*). Surprise me.

CARACTACUS (*smiling*). You's not
eatin' right. (*Shouts:*) You's not fit for
the war.

*And with one hand Caractacus lifts
the pool table up at one end, high.
Eddie dodges back, terrified.*

EDDIE. Don't do that! Don't do that! For
cryin' out loud!

*Eddie throws himself out of the way.
The light swinging badly. The big,
black form of the table topples over its*

*end. Caractacus stands in the
flickering light and shadow.*

CARACTACUS. I's going to get you *fit*
for the war!

EDDIE (*voice over*). Yeah. He'd changed
all right.

*And the drinkers burst back into the
room, almost falling over each other.
They freeze, staring at Eddie.*

CARACTACUS. No trouble. Mr Eddie
Cass here has just a lost a game of
pool. (*He laughs.*)

EDDIE. OK! OK! Get me fit.

CARACTACUS. Man you really want to
be fit – in all the God-given meanings
o' that little word? 'Fit' – that is
something else, 'fit' – 'fitness'.

EDDIE. I'll pay you.

A pause.

A thousand pound.

They stare at him.

I want to be a human bomb.

CARACTACUS (*gently*). No human
bomb. Maybe a human being.

First thing is to get you off the booze.

Cut at once to:

**28. Interior. Cramped space before a
toilet door.**

*Caractacus's friends are crowded around
Eddie. Caractacus has a bottle of Scotch.
He holds it up before Eddie's face.*

EDDIE. I don't think this is a good idea.

CARACTACUS. You're paying, man.

*He undoes the top of the bottle and
hands it to Eddie. With difficulty in
the cramped space they push Eddie
into the toilet.*

29. Interior. Toilet. Night.

*It's small. Eddie leans against the wall
exhausted. He looks at the whisky, then
at the pan.*

CARACTACUS (*off, from behind the
door*). Do it man!

*Eddie looks at the catch on the door.
Pauses. Then closes the catch and
drinks, desperately from the bottle.
Shouts outside – the door is banged.
Then hit. The catch bursts, the door
opens, they pile in. Eddie drinking
until the last moment. They take the
bottle from him.*

EDDIE. No. Please.

*And they hold his head down the
toilet, pouring the rest of the whisky
over him.*

Cut at once to:

30. Interior. Caractacus's place. Day.

*Up under the eaves of a building.
Mattresses on the floor – virtually bare.
Seen from floor level, Eddie is doing
press-ups. Jill is watching, cross-legged,
from a corner. Caractacus hitting the
floor beside Eddie, counting.*

CARACTACUS. Twenty-eight!
Twenty-nine! Thirty!

EDDIE. Please, please, can I die now?

31. Interior. Toilet. Night.

*Eddie alone, again with a bottle of
whisky. He looks at the bottle, the pan,
the door – hesitates – then drinks.
    And again, Caractacus and his friends
burst in.*

Cut at once to:

32. Interior. Toilet. Night.

*A few seconds later.
    Eddie's head being held down the pan;
whisky being poured over his head.*

Cut at once to:

33. Interior. Caractacus's place. Night.

*Jill again sitting in the corner watching –
as Caractacus throws a heavy medicine
ball into Eddie's stomach.
    He grunts. He falls backwards.*

Cut at once to:

34. Interior. Toilet. Night.

Caractacus's friends piling in a third time to a drinking Eddie, taking the bottle off him.

   Cut at once to:

35. Interior. Caractacus's place. Day.

Jill, lying on a mattress, smoking. Eddie is lifting weights, suffering. Caractacus lifting weights effortlessly.

   Cut at once to:

36. Interior. Toilet. Night.

Eddie looking at the bottle. With a sigh he pours the Scotch into the pan. The door swings open. Smiling faces.

37. Interior. Caractacus's place. Night.

Eddie and Caractacus boxing. Eddie getting the worse of it.

38. Interior. Pool room, back of the café. Night.

Eddie trying to lift the pool table by one hand. He manages it a little. A white and a black ball run down the table. He fails – drops the table. Jill, smoking at a table, laughs. Caractacus with a furious face.

39. Interior. Toilet. Night.

Eddie pouring Scotch down the pan. He stops. He leans against the wall.

EDDIE (*voice over*). It went on and on. Weeks it seemed. Like being underground.

He drinks a little of the whisky. At once the door flies open and Caractacus and his friends move in.

Oh God!

40. Interior. Caractacus's place. Night.

EDDIE. Thousand quid for this? I must be mad.

CARACTACUS. Just your body talkin'.

EDDIE. Like prison!

CARACTACUS. The body is a prison! But should be a temple.

EDDIE. What happened to you, Caractacus? You get religion or somethin'?

CARACTACUS. I had a flowering, Eddie, I had a flowering.

EDDIE. You what?

CARACTACUS (*close to his face*). I looked up. I was a weed, in the gutter. I decided – I will flower.

EDDIE. I see.

CARACTACUS. No you do not.

EDDIE. No?

CARACTACUS. Till it happen to you, one fair morning.

EDDIE. ?

He looks at Jill. She turns away, tetchily.

41. Interior. Toilet. Night.

Eddie pouring whisky away.

EDDIE (*voice over*). Whatever the light Caractacus had seen – Jesus, the revolution or whatever – he was beginnin' to work miracles for me.

Finished the bottle – drops it, casually, into the bowl.

42. Montage.

The training continues. With others. Judo and karate movements and holds. Boxing training. Head stands. Cartwheels. Now and then, Eddie and Caractacus playing 'knuckle'. Concentrate on the 'knuckle' – gets faster and faster.

EDDIE (*voice over*). Somethin' inside you – getting on the outside. You get so knackered then – you begin to turn inside out.

Music – the images of 'knuckle' between their fists coming very fast.

43. Interior. Pool room at the back of the café. Night.

It is crowded with Caractacus's friends, drinking at the tables. First, Caractacus lifts the table single-handed – a black and a white ball – they run down, hit each other and both go into the pockets.
  Silence. He puts the table back down.
  Eddie lifts the table, up and up – and over-turns it.
  The place goes wild with celebration.

44. Interior. Caractacus's place. Night.

Lit by table lamps on the floor. Eddie, Caractacus and Jill are looking at one of the walls of the room.
  It is a diagram, crudely but vividly drawn, like an elaborate graffiti, of the plot so far.
  The hatbox, the river – Stoker – the head of Hugo, with ear-ring, crossed out by a large cross. A face that's blacked out, 'the man' written above it. A figure with a bed and a horse on either side of her – 'Dana'.
  Arrows pointing to a figure – 'Eddie Cass'.
  They contemplate this display. The camera passes back and forth over it.
  They have pool cues – they point to the diagram.

CARACTACUS. So there is a man. There is a man.

Cue on the blacked-out head.

And this is your life! Mr Eddie Cass!

He laughs.

And this man – he has tastes, he has lusts.

The cue to Dana.

Like – your wife.

Look at Caractacus's face, then look at Eddie's.

And your wife's friend.

The murdered woman.

For this man o'power, he is a diver. He puts on his diving suit, and he goes down, deep, down –

Look at Caractacus's face.

Down to where you and I swim,

down in the deep sea. And this man he likes pretty fishes. He puts them on his hook.

The drawing of the murdered woman again.

He takes this fish out the water. And they die. Yes, man! We are living in one big tank. All this!

Cue round the whole diagram.

One big tank! He sends down his submarines, keep the fish quiet who say 'Hey, who is this, sending down hooks, cruel hooks among us! Hey up there!'

Cue to Hugo.

And the submarines, put out signs, on the bottom o' the tank saying – 'Be cool fish, it's one of you, going round, killing your own kind! Follow the poor little fish-head, in the river, fish! Swim after *him*! You got a shark among you. Name o' Eddie Cass.'

A pause. Look at Caractacus.

There are men doin' this to you, Eddie. Doing this to me. They got a wall, somewhere, in a big room, big house, underground bunker, in the works o' good old Big Ben for all we know – doin' this to you and me – so hard for us to contemplate. You's an arrow in the war-room, Eddie.

EDDIE. World War Three's goin' to break out. I promise you.

CARACTACUS. Boy, World War Three broke out long time ago. You'd know that if you was black.

They stare at each other.

EDDIE. Understand 'em. Got to – understand 'em.

Wipe to:

45. Interior. Caractacus's place. Night.

Same location. Later.
  Caractacus doing press-ups. Eddie cross-legged, with a chest-expander. Both puffing and sweating. They stop and look up at the wall. The blacked-out head of 'the man' looms above them.

JILL (*out of sight*). This is what it's like.

They look at her. She has been

drawing with felt-tipped, coloured markers on another wall.

It's a story I remember from when I was a kid.

Eddie and Caractacus crawl, looking childish, still panting, to stare at her drawing. Show it. It's an Indian village, tepees, stick-figure Indians, feathers, bows and arrows, like a children's drawing. Dominating the village is a totem pole, with monstrous heads.

(*Voice over, the camera moving about the drawing:*) Once upon a time there was an Indian village. In the middle of the village, was a totem pole. The totem pole was the Indians' god. So they loved it and worshipped it. But a witch had put a spell on the totem pole. At night, it walked about the village and began to murder the Indians.

Show a figure, lying down, drops of blood from it.

Then one night, two clever Indians stayed up, after the fires were out –

Show them, looking out from behind a tepee.

They saw the totem pole lift itself out of the ground and lumber about the village, and drag out an Indian from a tepee, while all the others were asleep, and kill. The two clever Indians were very afraid. They said 'If the whole village knows what is killing them, they'll go mad. They love the totem pole. They think it is everything that's good in the world.' So – they decided – to blame the murders – on someone else. There was an Indian –

Show a stick-figure, with a single feather on its head.

Whom people didn't like much –

EDDIE. You mean me.

CARACTACUS (*laughs*). Hiawatha, man! Or 'Hia-woops'.

JILL. Yeah, they blamed it on poor Hia-woops. And all the village believed them. And they stoned Hia-woops to death, and everyone was happy.

EDDIE. I see –

Show the head of 'the man'.

CARACTACUS (*voice over*). Totem pole.

Show Hugo and his companion, Eldridge, and the car.

Two clever Indians.

Show the Eddie drawing.

Hia-woops.

Eddie and Caractacus staring at the diagram.
A silence. The head of 'the man'

EDDIE. Who are you?

Eddie going close up to the drawing.

46. Interior. Caractacus's place. Night.

Jill and Eddie alone. One lamp. Shadows. Jill in the corner, smoking again. Eddie at another corner, staring at the diagram.

EDDIE. Can't you stop smokin'?

JILL. No.

She smokes.

EDDIE. Where you learn to draw?

JILL. Art college.

EDDIE. Oh yeah? You don't draw that good.

JILL. I left after a year.

EDDIE. Ah.

She chain-smokes another cigarette.

Please. I not been out f'weeks. Got all this fitness. In rooms. Somethin' called 'The Sky' out there, in't there?

JILL. Dunno.

EDDIE. Dunno? The sky. I wanna see if it's still there! Is it?

Jill eyeing him.

JILL. I discount all rumours.

EDDIE. How d'you mean?

She eyes him.

JILL. Who can you trust these days?

EDDIE. Your kind give me the creeps.

JILL. What kind?

EDDIE. See a lot o' you about. In the cities. All of you. Waiting around to die.

JILL. That what I'm doin'?

EDDIE. I seen your hand shake.

She puts her hand, with the cigarette, down.

JILL. Gettin' the big moralist are you? Now that you're 'fit'.

EDDIE. Waiting around to die. Like lizards.

JILL. Lizards –

She shrugs.

keep very still. They see a lot.

EDDIE. Yeah?

He loses interest, his eyes wandering over the diagram.

What you see?

JILL. Lizards don't say.

Caractacus comes in, fast.

CARACTACUS. Hey hey! Warrior! Hard man! Stoker!

EDDIE. What?

CARACTACUS. The brother who set you up!

EDDIE. Yeah?

He goes to the diagram.

CARACTACUS. The brother who set you up? The word is he's in Birmingham!

Eddie pointing at the drawings.

EDDIE (*voice over*). Understanding. Understanding what they're doin' to you.

The village, very briefly. The totem pole. The blacked-out head of 'the man'.

47. Interior. Caractacus's Cortina. Night.

Four of them driving.

48. Montage. Birmingham landscape. Night.

The blast of loud music. Birmingham, in stills and stock clips, the image spotty and coarse, violet-coloured.

EDDIE (*voice over*). Back to Birmingham that fair city, in Caractacus's beat up Cortina. Open sky again. Didn't seem like the sky. Beat up tin roof, over everythin', little holes for the stars.

Wipe to:

49. Exterior. Birmingham back street. Night.

*The Cortina parked by a wall. Stoker walking toward it, with a woman. Caractacus gets out of the Cortina. He carries a pool cue, in a plastic cue bag.
  He steps in front of Stoker and the woman.*

CARACTACUS. God go with you, sister.

She takes one look at Caractacus and steps back, then walks away, half-running.

STOKER. Hey –

CARACTACUS. Pool.

STOKER. ?

CARACTACUS. I want a game o' pool.

He holds the cue, in its bag, as a weapon. Flicks it against his leg.

STOKER. I don't play the game much, man.

CARACTACUS. Take me to the pool hall.

He indicates the car.

STOKER. Sure, sure.

He goes to get into the car. Sees Eddie. Reacts.

Oh no! No!

EDDIE. Hello Stoker. Got a parcel for me?

CARACTACUS. In!

JILL. I'll drive!

She runs round to the driver's seat and is getting in –

50. Montage. Motorway, the outskirts of Birmingham. Night.

The city glowing, overlaid stills and clips of the urban landscape at night, moving as if seen from a car.

51. Interior. Moving car. Night.

Jill driving. Caractacus in the back seat with Stoker. Eddie in the front seat.

STOKER. Hey Eddie I didn't mean nothing – man, since I did that little thing, my life's gone crazy. Crazy!

EDDIE. Tell us about it.

(*Voice over:*) I flooded wi' sweet feelings. Yeah, I'd been in a back of a car, shittin' myself witless. Yeah. Now I was in a front seat! All I needed was a front seat! All I needed was a little ear-ring on –

STOKER. Please! Look –

He looks at the others. He swallows.

They said, get you to do that. They gave me a grand!

EDDIE. Ha!

STOKER. A grand, just to give you a couple of addresses in a pub. And somethin' about a parcel. And they've never left me alone since!

EDDIE. Oh no?

STOKER. Told me to get out o' London, man! Birmingham, thought I'd be safe –

CARACTACUS. No one is safe, brother. The Lord sees all.

52. Exterior. Wasteground. Night.

Jill is at the wheel of the car. A good distance away, Eddie, Caractacus and Stoker. Go very close to them, Caractacus is sliding a pool cue out of its bag.

STOKER. Brother, I am weak, weak. I had – muscle thing, thing when I was a child. The rickets, you know? I had that.

EDDIE. They told you to get out of London. Who?

STOKER. Two guys. White. One – hair –

EDDIE. Fair hair!

STOKER. Right man!

EDDIE. Ear-ring. The other.

STOKER. Yeah! Yeah!

EDDIE. The other one.

STOKER. Heavy, heavy dude – big fruity voice. He was the one who came round.

EDDIE. Did he give you a name?

STOKER. Name?

CARACTACUS. Play some pool.

He caresses the handle of the cue.

EDDIE. Did you get his name? Was it Eldridge?

STOKER. No name.

EDDIE. How did you get in touch with him? Give you a 'phone number?

CARACTACUS. Peaceful game pool, like music. Comp-li-cated music.

STOKER. Yeah. London number. 073 0025.

Jill is walking toward them.

EDDIE. Address.

STOKER. No address –

CARACTACUS. On the table, violence of graceful music –

STOKER. All right! All right! This house, 13 –

JILL. That's enough, officer.

Jill has a gun and a small black wallet in the other hand.

STOKER. Oh thank God, thank God, thank God.

He sinks to his knees.

CARACTACUS (*shouts at Jill*). What you doing, bitch? Bitch?

JILL. Put that down.

CARACTACUS. You fooling me? You bitching me? You messing this whole operation?

JILL. Shut up and put that down!

CARACTACUS. You blowing it all! We gotta play along with Eddie – get out all he knows.

JILL (*to Caractacus*). Shut your mouth!

CARACTACUS (*to Jill*). This is way above your authority, man!

JILL. I said, shut your mouth!

STOKER. Authority? Hey – hey – I'm the policeman here?

JILL. Everyone shut up! I out rank everyone here!

CARACTACUS. Don't you bank on that, darlin'.

JILL. The operational orders are quite clear!

STOKER. What are you? The Bristol end of this operation? You are! You bastards! Hey, I know I be a mere detective-sergeant, but the way this operation's bein' run, man, I'm going to bust your bollocks! And yours!

JILL. Oh charming.

EDDIE. Er –

STOKER. You two are going to go *down*! I am going to put in a report!

EDDIE. What are you people?

JILL (*to Eddie*). Who can you trust these days? Tell him Caractacus. Tell him now.

CARACTACUS. Hey boy. (*Gently, reverting to the Caractacus of Episode 1.*) Hey.

Go very close to him and to Eddie. Tears in Caractacus's eyes.

They leant on me you see. That night, after you came back, with the mud of the river all over you. Hey. And they'd put her on to me, y'know? Knowing you were crashing with me –

53. Montage of flashbacks from Episode 1, Scene 26. Interior. Caractacus's flat.

A quick kaleidoscope of images from the scenes in Episode 1 – Eddie coming back to the basement flat, finding Caractacus and Jill in bed, then the police raid.

54. Exterior. Wasteground. Night.

CARACTACUS. Heavy. (*He pauses.*) Heavy. Those wallies, hey!

He laughs. Looks at Eddie pleadingly.

Don't know what you's into boy. Russians, perverts, spyin'. Don't know man.

But yeah, hey! They recruited me, hey, I'm a public servant.

I'm a dick, me, hey! That funny, hey? Me?

Hey boy, I'd like to kiss you, jus' on the head, you mind if I do that? My old friend, my old comrade-in-arms, all them piddling jobs down in Peckham we did, hey?

And here we are on the other side o' the moon, and me a paid-up policeman and you –

He reaches out to kiss Eddie who recoils.

Judas time.

A silence.

They said they'd bring you down to Bristol. Did, didn't she. Debriefing man. What you knew.

A flash of the diagram on the wall from Episode 3, Scene 44.

Great to see you again it were, Eddie – boy. Hey. I'm goin' to get a pension, y'know? This thieving and – knocking out alsation dogs the back o' garages.

You do the same boy. Settle down. Hey Eddie, my friend –

A soft pumping sound. Caractacus's face is still. Then his mouth opens and blood gushes out. Look at them from a distance. Caractacus silently is on the ground, his body contorting. Stoker has thrown himself aside. Eddie backs away from Jill, who stands there calmly, holding the silenced gun.

JILL (*her voice more middle-class than before, calm*). Traduced. Do you know what that word means, Eddie Cass? It is what's happening to you. 'Traduced.'

Eddie backs away. Look at the group, from his view as he does so – breathing heavily. She calls out as he retreats.

And look what you've done now. Killed your best friend? That what you done, Eddie? Eddie? What have you done?

55. Interior. Dim public library. Murky light.

Down-and-out men and women, hunched over the brown tables, reading newspapers. A single librarian sits on a chair. Eddie sneaks around the library, glances at the librarian – she yawns.

*Echoey sound, street. A shuffle, the
squeak of a chair. He goes to the
full-volume edition of the* Oxford English
Dictionary. *He runs a grubby finger along
the worn spines of the books. He finds
'tr –'. He takes out the volume and puts it
on a table.*
    *Close to the pages – he turns it and
finds 'traduced'.*
    *Look at the words as he runs his finger
along them.*

EDDIE (*voice over, muttering to
    himself*). Traduce.
    To lead across –
    Lead along as a spectacle, to bring into
    disgrace. To –

His finger wanders down.

Speak evil of, falsely, defame, malign,
slander, to dishonour – disgrace.

*He pauses. His finger slides from the
page. He slams the book shut. The
librarian is suddenly awake, sitting
bolt-upright. Eddie shouts.*

Not me! Not me, not any longer!

*He throws the book. It hits the
librarian full in her face. She goes
backwards with a scream. He bumps
his way out of the library.*

**56. Exterior. Montage of streets,
pavements, corners as used earlier in
this episode. Running along them,
corner after corner, the music blasting.
Then suddenly – Eddie against a wall
hitting the brick with his fist.**

EDDIE. Not me! Not me! Not me!

Look at his fist – covered in blood.

End of Episode 3.

*And over the credits the heavy-metal
rendering of:*

Pussycat pussycat
Where have you been?
I've been to London
To see the Queen.

Pussycat pussycat
What did you there?
I frightened a mouse
Under her chair.

Episode 4

The Patriot

Episode 4

Characters

EDDIE CASS	Denis Lawson
DANA	Lindsay Duncan
ELDRIDGE	George Baker
ANGELA	Leonie Mellinger
THE MAN	Ernest Clark
TEDDY	Tim Potter
YOUNG MAN	John Ainley
SECURITY GUARDS	Ned Kelly
	Barry Ewart
POLICEMEN	Stephen Oxley
	Michael Shallard
1ST TELEPHONE VOICE	Carrie Lee Baker
2ND TELEPHONE VOICE	Stephen Oxley

i EDDIE: 'And I got lucky. There he was. Bags of bonhomie.'

ii ELDRIDGE: 'Why, Mr Eddie Cass, our bad penny.'

iii ANGIE: 'He's nicked a tank! He always wanted to.'

iv EDDIE: 'They've got all the guns. Tanks. They've even got tanks.'

v DANA: 'He's in Glasgow. Opening something, quite a lot. Y'know. Big deals.'

vi EDDIE and the second hatbox.

vii MAN: 'It would be very much to your advantage if you would allow me to intrude for a moment.'

1. Blank Screen.

EDDIE (*voice over*). Funny what it does to you.

A pause.

To read in the papers that you are dead.

2. Front page of the 'DAILY EXPRESS'.

Headline: 'THAMES HORROR KILLER – DEAD.' Two pictures: the hatbox and Caractacus.
Eddie's hand touches Caractacus's picture. He reads:

EDDIE (*reading*). 'Scotland Yard spokesman said that Christian Beloy, known as 'Caractacus' in London's underworld, was found dead in Birmingham. Police had suspected him of the Thames headless corpse murder and were to make an arrest. Beloy left a suicide note, confessing to the brutal sexual killing of Mary Campbell, 20, in Peckham, South London, last –'

At once to Eddie's face.

What they doing?

What is this?

3. Interior. Train buffet. Night.

As in Episode 3: It is full of lumbering, half-drunk men. Eddie sits at a table clutching an orange juice, the now tattered Daily Express *in his hands. Caractacus's picture stares up at him.*

4. Flashback to Episode 3, Scenes 46 and 52.

A flash of Jill saying 'Who can you trust these days?' in Caractacus's room. Then the same line at once on the wasteground in Birmingham.

5. Interior. Train: buffet. Night.

EDDIE (*voice over*). And that horrible thought came to me. (*Aloud, shouts –*

hitting the buffet table, drinks bouncing:) They don't know what they're doin'!

The drinkers stare at him.

6. Interior. Pay-phone, bar. Night.

Eddie pushes coins in the box.

PHONE VOICE. Capital Radio.

EDDIE. Hello, Capital?

PHONE VOICE. Capital Radio, can I help you?

EDDIE. I wanna go on a phone in!

A brief pause.

PHONE VOICE. Just hold the line, please –

Another voice at once.

Late night call, what do you want to ask?

EDDIE. This headless murder.

PHONE VOICE (*at once*). Yes.

EDDIE. I didn't do it.

PHONE VOICE. Yes.

EDDIE. But they said I did!

PHONE VOICE (*slight pause*). Yes.

EDDIE. I was there – when they shot – the, the bloke they said did do it!

PHONE VOICE. So what question do you want to ask?

EDDIE. I – just wanna tell someone!

PHONE VOICE. I'm afraid that all the calls are really piled up tonight, do you think you could call again, perhaps tomorrow?

Eddie, tears in his eyes. He slams the telephone down.

7. The Daily Express building, Fleet Street. Night.

The glassy front looms up.

8. Interior. Reception area of the Daily Express building. Night.

Three very large security men are struggling with Eddie.

EDDIE. I gotta tell the editor! 'Bout my life!

1ST SECURITY MAN. First one tonight!

2ND SECURITY MAN. Out you go, friend. Back in the pub.

NB, these little scenes are very short, to be edited very tightly, flick in and out of them.

9. Interior. Police Station. Night.

Two policemen behind a desk.

EDDIE (*in mid flow*). Right there! Before my eyes! They did it! See?

Waves the now shredded Daily Express.

So! So! I wanna make a complaint! Why don't you want to arrest *me*! Why you all stopped goin' for *me*!

1ST POLICEMAN. All right. On your way.

Eddie hits him in the face.

2ND POLICEMAN (*moving fast*). Oh *no*!

10. Interior. Police cell. Night.

Eddie, sitting dead still. Staring at the wall. Look at him from a distance. Jump to closer to him.

11. Insert flashback to Episode 3, Scene 52.

STOKER. Yeah. London number. 073 0025.

Jill is walking toward them. And cut to a few seconds later in the clip.

All right! All right! This house, 13 –

12. Interior. Police cell. Night.

EDDIE (*voice over*). Eldridge.

Jump to close to him. He is dead still. Then springs up and is hammering the door.

(*Aloud, shouting:*) Phone book! Get me a phone book! I want a phone book!

Door opening and – the 2nd policeman is there.

2ND POLICEMAN. Now! (*he pauses.*) Get your possessions at the desk and out.

EDDIE. What? Not going to do me for assault?

2ND POLICEMAN. Out.

EDDIE. Make a call, did you? Someone tell you – kick him out?

2ND POLICEMAN (*close*). Now look, this is the beginning of a long night –

EDDIE. All right. Proves it though, don't it! Don't it!

2ND POLICEMAN. Look, you are just one more looney, now –

13. Exterior. Telephone box. Night.

Inside Eddie is going through the telephone books.

14. Interior. Telephone box. Night.

Same location. Eddie is going through the telephone directory, muttering.

EDDIE. 1296, 727, house number 13, lucky, luck numbers, 1296 –

Wipe to:

15. Interior. Telephone box. Night.

Same location. Later. Eddie is going through the numbers, muttering. Two men outside. One shrugs and gives up. The other knocks. Eddie pulls the door open in a fury.

EDDIE. I'm lookin' up a number. All right? All right?

The man nods and backs away.

16. Interior. Telephone box. Night.

Later. Eddie tearing out pages up to his knees in them. Exhausted, he finds the address.

EDDIE (*reading*). 13 Holland Park
   Crescent. Name – A – G – Cranmer.

Look at his face. Tears in his eyes.

**17. Insert. Flashback to Episode 3,
Scene 45. The drawing of the Indian
village from Episode 3.**

*The camera moves from totem pole to the
murdered Indian, to the two Indians
looking from behind the tepee then, not
shown in Episode 3, a group of Indians
fighting amongst themselves. Then two
making love.*
The drawing blisters.

18. Exterior. Holland Park. Dawn.

*Eddie wakes, shivering. He looks about
him. The park is misty.*

EDDIE (*voice over*). Looney. In the park.
   Counted the houses along.

*The backs of large houses, over a wall
with gate doors.*

Nine, eleven, thirteen. Built like prisons
when you see 'em from the back.
Alarms, TV cameras. But not to keep
'em in, to keep loonies like me out. I
was so tired I'd gone right through it,
out the other side. I felt like I was
walking on water. Any moment – I
could just sort o' bend my legs in a
certain way, and fly. Fly away.

*A young woman, later known as
Angela, comes out of a gate door in
the wall. She wears a light mackintosh
and a headscarf. She is seen from a
long way away, Eddie stands.*

19. Exterior. Park. Day.

Travelling shot. Eddie follows Angela.

20. Interior. Coach. Dawn.

Mist.
   *In a mews, a scruffy old coach – curly
body lines, scratched paint. On it a CND
sign and the slogan:*
   Animate liberals.

*The woman disappearing into the
coach. The door slides shut. Eddie looks
at the slogan.*

EDDIE (*to himself*). Bloody hell, what's
   this lot then?

*He peers into the coach, cannot see
anything.*

21. Interior. Coach. Day.

*Eddie tears the door of the coach open
and rushes in. He falls over boxes, cans
of food, fur rugs, broken guitars. Angela
and a young man with long hair look up.
He is naked, on an old brown, fur rug;
she is half-undressed.*

**22. Insert. Flashback to Episode 4,
Scene 17.**

*A quick flash – The two Indians making
love in the drawing.*

23. Interior. Coach. Day.

*Eddie, lifting the naked young man up
under his armpits.*

EDDIE. Out, toe-rag!

YOUNG MAN. Y'what –

EDDIE. This is a bust! I am your evil
   fairy grandmother!

YOUNG MAN. This coach is cool! I
   made it legal! It's MOT'd!

EDDIE. Out! Out!

YOUNG MAN. Let me get my clothes
   then –

*The young man grabs his clothes.
Eddie pulls the door open, throws him
out. The young man, at the door.*

YOUNG MAN. I got a lot o'mates!
   They're a lot of us on the road! They'll
   screw you!

EDDIE. Out!

Eddie pulls the door shut.

ANGELA (*upper-class*). What a
   hard man.

EDDIE. All right. And what's your rank?

ANGELA. How do you mean?

EDDIE. Don't you give me that! Don't give me that!

ANGELA. 'Rank'? Are you in the Army, or something? My boyfriend's in the Army.

EDDIE. That toe-rag?

ANGELA (*laughs*). Oh not *him*!

EDDIE. What is he then?

ANGELA. Oh he's just – you know. Actually you had better think over what he said. He has a lot of friends. And hippies aren't what they were in the sixties, love and flowers. This lot are really vicious little rats.

EDDIE. What you doin' with them then?

ANGELA (*shrugs*). Fun. And, you know, they give us – stuff. For our lot.

EDDIE. Lot?

ANGELA (*laughs*). 'Set' I think they used to say.

EDDIE. Tell me about your set.

ANGELA. Oh some of them are quite brilliant, you'd be surprised.

EDDIE. Yeah? M.I.5?

ANGELA. Don't know about that. How does anyone know what anyone is?

EDDIE. Where you live. That house.

ANGELA. What do you mean?

EDDIE. 13, Holland Park Crescent.

ANGELA (*pale*). How do you know my address?

EDDIE. Come on! You're one of 'em!

ANGELA. You must never go there. Never, ever, ever, Daddy will kill me!

EDDIE. What's your Daddy's name?

ANGELA. You don't know?

EDDIE. Eldridge.

ANGELA. No. Lord Cranmer.

EDDIE. Oh Yeah?

ANGELA. I mean, Daddy bought the house in Holland Park as his second *pied-à-terre*, and lets me stay there, as long as I don't bring – you know, anything back with me.

EDDIE. Anything?

ANGELA. You know. Anyone.

EDDIE. Fool about, do you? Like with the toe-rag?

ANGELA. I get bored a lot.

EDDIE. Right. See how this bores you.

24. Interior. Coach. Day.

Montage.
Angela in different positions in the coach, as Eddie talks to her. Examine her face, indifferent, enigmatic.

EDDIE (*voice over*). Told her what they'd done to me.

Thought, am I gonna be condemned, tellin' this, all my life? To that look?

Eyes goin' down.

In a face I can't read.

In a country I can't understand.

On some kind o' quest. I didn't know what for.

Wipe to:

25. Interior. Coach. Day.

Later.

EDDIE. So. Tell me you don't believe me.

Angela makes a dash for the door. He grabs her, throws her back over the rugs.

ANGELA (*terrified*). Did – didn't you see the papers this morning?

Eddie stares. She grabs her mackintosh, takes out a Daily Telegraph. *Unfolds it, points to a story on the front page.*

26. Daily Telegraph.

The headline: 'HEADLESS WOMAN'S BODY – BARNES COMMON'.
It blisters.

27. Montage. Flashback to Episode 3, Scenes 44 and 45.

The black head of the diagram, the totem pole of the drawing.

EDDIE (*voice over*). Again. Again. He's done it again.

Cut at once to:

28. Interior. The coach. Day.

EDDIE (*to himself*). Oh God I hope its not Dana. Oh God let it not be Dana.

Angela makes a dive at the door again. He pulls her back. He starts the engine of the coach.

Where is this Daddy of yours?

ANGELA. I –

EDDIE. Where!

ANGELA. Away. In the country.

EDDIE. Right! Bored are you, darlin'? Right! Where –

ANGELA. House party –

EDDIE. Off we go!

29. Interior. The coach. Day.

Eddie driving. Angela comes and sits next to him.

ANGELA. Say I believe you, then.

EDDIE. You believe me.

ANGELA. Wouldn't it be fun if Daddy was mixed up in this.

EDDIE. Yeah?

ANGELA. Wouldn't it be fun, actually – if Daddy was the man!

EDDIE. What is it with your dad? Hate his guts do you?

ANGELA. No. Yes. Whatever passes the time.

EDDIE (*shouts*). What's gettin' to people. What's a matter with 'em!

ANGELA. Just the end of the world, isn't it. Haven't you noticed? It's getting to everyone. People are blowing up.

EDDIE. Oh yeah?

ANGELA. All the time.

30. Exterior. The coach, parked. Day.

The coach parked off the verge of a minor road, under trees.

31. Interior. Coach. Day.

Eddie and Angela eating baked beans from tins, with spoons.

ANGELA. Mm! Mm! Isn't this fun?

EDDIE. Huh.

ANGELA. Do you want some smack?

EDDIE. What?

ANGELA. The coach is packed with it.

EDDIE. Yeah?

ANGELA. That mean yes?

EDDIE. No, it means – I don't know about you. *At all.*

ANGELA. Don't get boring, Eddie. Whatever you do. Don't get boring and I'll be all right.

EDDIE. Oh. OK.

32. Interior. Coach. Day.

Later.
  Angela and Eddie have made love. The furs around them. He cradles her.

EDDIE. We better move. Don't want some local bobby on his bike, findin' the bus –

ANGELA. Don't worry. There's no one else alive out there.

EDDIE. No?

ANGELA. No. The neutron bomb went off. Didn't you notice?

EDDIE. Why are we still here then?

ANGELA (*softly*). We aren't. We aren't.

EDDIE. Dear oh dear!

He gets up, pulling his shirt on.

Get goin'.

ANGELA. Don't worry, we're very near there now.

Close to her. Tears in her eyes.

33. Exterior. Coach in the countryside. Late afternoon.

Eddie stepping out of the coach, Angela behind him. He looks out.

EDDIE. I should've known it.

34. Exterior. Country house. Day.

With a blast of music, what Eddie sees – nestling amongst the fields and woods, above a lake, the country house of Episode 2.

EDDIE (*voice over*). You be all right here?

ANGELA (*voice over*). Why not? Not falling in love with me or something, are you?

EDDIE (*voice over*). Neutron-bombed out o' me, years ago. Sorry. 'Love'.

ANGELA (*voice over*). I'll be all right.

35. Exterior. Country house. Day.

Music. Eddie running down toward the distant country house.

36. Exterior. Country house. Day.

Music. Eddie running down toward the distant country house.

37. Exterior. Country house. Night.

The windows ablaze with light, the front door open, light pouring down the steps and across the driveway. In the windows and up and down the steps, men in evening dress, women in gowns. The sound of music from within – Schubert.

EDDIE (*voice over*). Lords and masters. Lords and masters.

38. Exterior. Bushes and trees. Night.

Eddie moves amongst the bushes, looking out.

39. Exterior. Country house steps and driveway. Night.

Eldridge comes down the steps. He is a little drunk. He smokes a cigar. Seen from Eddie's view.

EDDIE (*voice over*). Eldridge.

Eldridge stands on the driveway smoking.

EDDIE (*low*). Come on, come on, you bastard. Please. Please.

Eldridge yawns and lumbers toward the bushes. He opens his fly and urinates. Eddie stands up in front of him. They stare at each other.

ELDRIDGE. Why. Mr Eddie Cass. Our bad penny.

He reaches for a gun inside his dress-suit. Eddie flies at him.

Cut to:

40. Exterior. Bushes and trees. Night.

Grunts, a struggle, ugly and awkward – Eddie with his fist in Eldridge's mouth, holding the gun to his throat. Montage this half-dragging, deeper into woodland.

EDDIE (*voice over*). On and on. Dragged him. At last I'd got my hands on one. After all the dance they'd led me. And he had teeth, and he could choke, and he was half-pissed, and his bowels had gone I realised, after a while, and he was just – flabby meat. And shit-scared.

41. Exterior. Countryside – edge of a field. Night.

In the middle-distance, the country house, its lights blazing. Eddie takes his fist out of Eldridge's mouth.

ELDRIDGE. Please. No more. No – my heart, bad, I. Please. Rest.

EDDIE (*close to his face*). Sh. Sh.

Close to their faces – they look at each other.

42. Flashback to Episode 1, Scenes 28 and 30.

Flashes of Eldridge in the car from Episode 1. The pistol coming at Eddie's face.

43. Exterior. Edge of a field. Night.

Eldridge lying in Eddie's lap.

EDDIE. Why do you let me go all the time? Why do you let me run?

44. Flashback to Episode 2, Scene 69 and Episode 3, Scene 54.

Very briefly – from Episode 2, Hugo being shot in the field. From Episode 3, Caractacus being shot, Jill lowering her gun.

45. Exterior. Edge of a field. Night.

ELDRIDGE. Sport.

EDDIE. What?

ELDRIDGE (*coughing*). Good sport, old chap.

EDDIE. You what?

46. Flashback to Episode 2, Scene 64.

The hunt assembling.

47. Exterior. Edge of a field. Night.

ELDRIDGE. Oh yes.

A laugh, a cough.

Can't touch you, you see.

EDDIE. How d' you mean?

ELDRIDGE. Your lovely wife. She's your protector. She found out – what we were up to. You know that amusing little jaunt –

EDDIE. Jaunt?

ELDRIDGE. The head in the river? Yes. You were a good candidate. I mean – there was a connection with the girl and your wife, to you – looked lovely. Then – your Dana, my dear Eddie, became more and more favoured.

EDDIE. By the man.

ELDRIDGE. So – so –

Short breath.

We who are but the lavatory cleaners in this matter – were thrown into disarray. Having set out to, to –

EDDIE. Traduce. That's the word. Who is he? The man? He's done it again han't he! Killed another girl.

ELDRIDGE. Yes, yes. Heavy days at the office.

He laughs, coughs.

EDDIE. What you going to do 'bout that one then? Eh?

Laughs.

ELDRIDGE. The committee will meet. Brilliant men – will be brilliant. Young men and women will go out into the country. The cities. All will be – maintained. The bingo winners in the popular dailies will be announced on time, and paid. The team – for the next winter cricket tour will be picked.

EDDIE. Who is he? The man.

ELDRIDGE. Don't you know? Can't you guess?

He begins to cry.

EDDIE (*hysterical*). You want me to beat it out, torture it out o' you? You want me to do that?

Shaking Eldridge.

Who! Who! Who you all runnin' about all over England for!

A gurgling sound from Eldridge – a heart attack.

What?

Ear close to the gurgling Eldridge.

ELDRIDGE (*a horrible, bubbling sound*). Pussycat, Pussycat –

A laugh that turns into a grimace and a look of terror.
Eddie backs away.

EDDIE. Who?

Goes into the dark.

(*Low:*) Who, who –

Eldridge left alone, sudden flood of moonlight, he contorts and dies.

48. Exterior. Countryside. Night.
Eddie running. Blast of music. Briefly:

49. Interior. Coach. Night.
Eddie wrenches the door open, throws himself into the driving seat.

EDDIE. Ange!

He starts the engine. Looking over his shoulder.

Ange!

She is at the back, heavily stoned.

Oh God! Zombies! Zombies!

50. Exterior. A wood. Day.
The coach parked. Bird-song. Eddie comes out of the coach.

51. Exterior. By the coach door. Day.
Close on Eddie.

TEDDY (*not seen in the bracken. Upper-class voice*). Hello there, old chap.

Eddie looks, a smiling Teddy is laying on the ground, a Sten gun trained on Eddie.

EDDIE. Oh.

TEDDY. Been keeping Angie warm for me have you, old chap? She tells me your charabanc here is loaded to the seams with lovely smack.

ANGELA (*coming out of the coach*). Teddy! Teddy!

They embrace, rolling, the Sten gun waves in the air.

52. Exterior. Wood. Day.
A just-killed rabbit. In Teddy's hands a knife flashes. The rabbit's entrails gush.

TEDDY. Did this with bloody sheep in The Falklands you know.

ANGELA (*to Eddie*). Isn't he marvellous?

EDDIE (*closes his eyes*). Oh God.

53. Exterior. Wood. Evening.
A camp fire, the rabbit skinned and burning on a stick. A billycan, frothing. Teddy, Angela and Eddie round the fire.

TEDDY. If what you say is so, then there's a big man, looked up to in public, probably on TV all the time, pontificating, and a rather nasty nest of minders. Who seem to be running their own organisation to look after him, procure him women, and cover up when he goes ape over said women.

Eddie stares at Teddy.

EDDIE. Yeah! Yeah!

TEDDY. Disgusting. You know, the Army in this country has nothing to do with politics. 'Less it's doing the Micks over. Or the wogs. Or the looney left if they got so bold. The Army's absolutely above politics altogether. Have some meat. Tell you what, what if we sprinkle some of that smack over it? Kind of marinade, ha! ha!

EDDIE. Er. Not for me.

He is handed a piece of rabbit. He bites it, spits it out.

This is raw!

TEDDY. That's the point of field cooking. Toughens you up.

Eddie spitting.

But what you tell me sounds like something terrible. Right in the body politic. Tell you what I'll do. I've got a few friends in Army Intelligence. I'll ask 'em if they've got a whiff of this. May put 'em on to it. Give me two days. Then we'll rendezvous. See what we can do. Now –

Look at him – he sniffs drugs.

I say. How much of this can I take off you? There's a terrible famine in the regiment right now, for stuff of this quality.

EDDIE. Have it all. I mean – we got to look after our heroes, haven't we.

TEDDY. What? Oh. Yes.

Gives Eddie a hard look.

Two days.

54. Exterior. Derelict buildings (the coach). Day.

Eddie and Angela, a distance apart, turning around slowly.

EDDIE (*voice over*). Outskirts o' Glasgow. Two days later. Glasgow. Where the first girl came from. The great rottin' city o' the North. Glasgow.

EDDIE (*speaks*). Why here? There's nothing here.

ANGELA. The Army can go anywhere. Or Teddy's bit of it can.

She laughs. A rumbling noise. A tank bursts out of a ramshackle outhouse.

EDDIE. Jesus Christ!

ANGELA. He's nicked a tank! He always wanted to!

EDDIE. The bloody cavalry, eh?

The tank stops. The gun begins to turn – toward Eddie.

EDDIE. Er –

He takes a step back, then walks the other way. The barrel of its gun follows him. He stops. The gun stops and begins to lower. Eddie, his mouth open.
  Teddy climbs up out of the top of the tank. A megaphone in his hand. He is wildly stoned.

TEDDY (*megaphone*). Traitor! You are a traitor!

ANGELA. Teddy! What fun!

She runs to the tank and climbs up to join Teddy.

TEDDY (*megaphone*). You are an Argie, Mick, wog, lefty traitor!

EDDIE. Cut it out!

Angela, laughing, is helped down into the tank by Teddy – the hatch closes.
  Eddie alone with the tank. He backs away. The tank begins. It chases him, he runs.

Wipe to:

55. A broad panorama, Glasgow at sunset.

The musical blast.

EDDIE (*voice over*). Always back to the cities. A rat must know his hole, eh?

56. Exterior, In the Gorbals. Night.

A levelled area of rubble, flat, dusty. Lights on a tall block of flats, dominating it. A broken pavement runs alongside the flat area. Eddie is discovered sitting on the area, drinking heavily.
  Leery music.

EDDIE (*voice over*). All the guns.

When he speaks, his speech is slurred. The voice overs are not.

(*Speaks:*) They got all the guns!

(*Voice over:*) Tanks.

(*Speaks:*) They rrr even g' tanks! Tanks!

(*Voice over:*) Black cars. Houses. Field. Barbed wire. Cameras on walls.

(*Speaks:*) Cameras, everywh–where!

(*Voice over:*) In trees.

(*Speaks:*) Inna trees –

(*Voice over:*) They can pick us off, anytime.

(*Speaks:*) Cut off our heads. Off w'my head!

He blinks, seeing something. Above a dark building, a neon sign – 'Citizens' Theatre'.

57. Exterior. Outside the Citizens' Theatre, Glasgow. Night.

Eddie lurches along the pavement. A theatre audience is coming out of the theatre. The play advertised is 'Dangerous Corner'. His knees go – he is a classic drunk. He blinks at the crowd and catches a glimpse of Dana, fur coat, hair tight and glistening, diamond ear-rings flashing. A chauffeur is ushering her toward – the big black car. He loses sight of her.

EDDIE (*voice over*). Dana.

(Speaks, hopelessly slurred:) Da –
DA – n – n – Da –

*The car is driving toward him. He
stands waving, the bottle in one hand.
It drops and smashes. The car passes
him, very close to the pavement. He
falls on all fours. Close to his face.
Catches his breath. Looks back over
his shoulder. The car has stopped.
He grunts.*

No. No. The man. No. No.

*The chauffeur gets out of the car and
runs towards him. Eddie cowers. The
chauffeur, face unseen beneath his
peaked cap, hands Eddie a slip of
paper. Scrawled hurriedly on it –
DANA – and an address.*

58. Exterior. Derelict tenement. Dawn.

*Eddie, in a terrible state, looks up. Looks
at the slip of paper again. Frowns.*

59. Interior. Tenement stairway. Dawn.

*Eddie climbing it. Rubbish, bricks, bottles
everywhere. His foot crunches on
something. Look down. It's a hypodermic
needle. He goes to a door. Consults the
scrap of paper. Pushes the door, it opens.*

**60. Interior. Filthy room. Tenement.
Day.**

*Part of the wall is bashed in and open to
the sky. Eddie alone in the room. A door
swings open to the sky. Eddie is alone in
the room. A door swings open. Dana
comes in, still wearing the fur coat.*

DANA. Come on! In 'ere!

*He follows her through the door. It is
a small room, the window with
hardboard over it. A camp bed, but
with fluffy white fur and soft toys
covering it. A candelabrum on an
orange-box. Champagne in an
ice-bucket.*

EDDIE. Wh – love nest?

DANA. No. I try to get these places.
When he moves about y'know. To get
away. They know about 'em perhaps,

but – let me do it. For a bit of home.

Look at her. Her eyes are tired.

Want some shampoo?

Indicating the champagne.

He's in Glasgow. Opening something,
quite a lot. Y'know. Big deals. So!

An attempt at a girlish gesture.

I've had this hidey-hole, off and on.

EDDIE. Who is he?

DANA. Yeah. Always openin' things
up here. S'spose 'cos the city's such a
shit heap.

Losing her drift.

In't it terrible, the unemployment, what
do you think should be done?

She plomps down on the bed.

EDDIE. What you talkin' about? Who
is the bastard? Tell me, I'll kill 'im
for you –

A look of pity from her.

DANA. I want to tell you.

She pauses.

I will.

She pauses.

But –

Her breath a little short.

But I got to go now. Come back.
Tonight. Yes, Eddie?

EDDIE. No. No. You stay where you are!

DANA. You don't realise –

EDDIE. God so help me, I'll – bash his
name out of you!

DANA. You can't hurt me. Compared to
him. Do you want to see – the skin on
my back?

EDDIE *(low)*. Oh Jesus.

DANA *(looking down, oddly bright)*. But
the unemployment is so bad, what *is*
your solution?

*He goes to lift her by the arm. She
scampers away, over the bed. They
stare at each other.*

NO! *(She pauses.)* Come back. I'll tell
you. I will. I will.

*She runs out of the door. He runs after
her.*

61. Interior. Tenement stairway. Day.

*Dana's shadow disappearing down it.
Eddie stumbles. He leans back against
the railing. He looks down. The dirty
floor, the dirty wall – they blister.*

62. Blank screen.

*Men's low voices, the words inaudible.
Feet going down the stairwell, quickly.*

63. Interior. Tenement stairway. Night.

*Eddie wakes with a start. Turns, looking
down the stairway. Almost catches sight
of a shadow, going down.*

EDDIE. Dana?

He stands, runs down the stairway.

Dana? Dana?

*He stops, then looks up. Leery music.
He climbs the stairway. Goes to the
door – slowly and fearfully.*

64. Interior. Tenement room. Night.

*City lights from the hole in the wall,
casting shadows on his face. There is
flickering candlelight from under the door
of the little inner room. He goes to it –
and kicks it open. Candlelight in his face.*

65. Interior. Small tenement room. Night.

*What Eddie sees.
   The candelabrum alight on the orange-
box. On the fur covered bed, a leather
hatbox.
   Zoom to the hat-box. Then, Eddie's
face.
   And from Eddie's point of view,
approach the box. His hands on it,
shaking violently. He fumbles the lid off.
Look up at Eddie's face, which contorts
to a scream.
   Smeared, hazy wipe to:*

66. Interior. Small Tenement room. Night.

*Same location. A few minutes later.
   The hatbox is open on the bed. Eddie is
crouched in a corner, shivering with
shock, mouth open, unable to scream.
Suddenly a voice from the other room –
full, fruity, upper-class, a man's.*

MAN. Mr Cass, would you come out here
please.

*Eddie's shivering stops. He stares at
the door.*

Mr Cass, it would be very much to
your advantage, if you would come out
here, please.

Eddie slowly approaches the door.

67. Interior. First tenement room. Night.

*A superb, blazing gas lamp – throwing its
harsh and shadowy light on a tall, slim,
beautifully dressed, sun-tanned, smiling
middle-aged man, with silvery,
beautifully cut hair.*

EDDIE. You –

MAN. No, no, Mr Cass, you understand
nothing. I am not the man you seek.
The sad, desperate, dear man, whose –
terrible misfortunes you have become
embroiled within.

*Eddie, thrown by the man's effortless
authority.*

EDDIE. Misfortunes? *His* – misfortunes?
with that – thing in there, he's got mis–

MAN. Indeed he has. We who are close
to him, look upon it as a curse. But he
will be cured. We hope and pray so –
and that your wife's death will be the
last. There is hope.

EDDIE. Hope?

MAN. Now I am going to tell you
his name.

*He leans to Eddie and whispers in his
ear. We do not hear the name.
   Look at Eddie's face, his eyes wide.*

EDDIE. Oh.

A silence.

Oh.

A silence.

I see.

A silence.

Well.

A silence.

I –

He suddenly sits down. He looks up. The man's smiling face looming above him.

I mean o' course, in that case –

MAN. I know you are a patriotic man. For reasons of State, of National Security, I know that you can be counted on.

EDDIE. Course. Queen an' country.

The man offers Eddie a cigarette from a gold case. A wipe, to the sound of crashing waves, and shingle:

68. Exterior. Blazing sunshine. A beach in the Bahamas.

Eddie sits at a white table beneath a gaily coloured sun umbrella. He is in beach shorts, his chest deeply tanned and with flashy gold chains and medalions around his neck. He holds an exotic drink in one hand and a cigar in the other.

EDDIE. Appealed to my patriotism. So that was the end of my quest. Never knew who the girl – you know, the head – in the hat-box were. Thank God it weren't Dana. She's here with me now. There she is.

Dana in bikini and dark glasses runs into shot. She waves.

DANA. Hello!

EDDIE. She does the hotel books.

DANA. Yeah, I do.

EDDIE. Oh yeah. H.M. Government did us well. Bahamas. Nice little hotel. A quarter of a million, nice nest egg. I mean, I'd do anything for my country.

He puts the cigar in his mouth. He grins.

Toodle-ooh. Say goodbye Dana.

DANA. Bye.

Tropical musak.

The end.